BLACK
IN THE
MIDDLE

BLACK IN THE MIDDLE

An Anthology of the Black Midwest

Edited by Terrion L. Williamson

First Edition 2020
ISBN: 978-1-948742-69-6

Belt Publishing
3143 W. 33rd Street, Cleveland, Ohio 44109
www.beltpublishing.com

Book design by Meredith Pangrace & David Wilson
Cover design by David Wilson
Cover photograph by Njaimeh Njie

BLACK MIDWEST INITIATIVE

The Black Midwest Initiative was launched in the fall of 2017 with the mission of speaking to the dearth of attention given to the complexities of black Midwestern life within the national media, institutions of higher education, the creative arts, and elsewhere. As a platform, we are interested in highlighting the ongoing work people are doing, whether academic, creative, or organizational, that speaks to the experiences of people of African descent living within the Midwest and the larger industrial sector of the U.S. As a progressive collective of people both within and beyond the academy who are dedicated to the cause of social justice, we are deeply invested in attending to issues that affect a whole range of people who identify as black or of African descent, including those who are poor and working class, women or non-binary, Muslim, LGBTQIA, immigrant, and disabled. As individuals who hail from and/or currently live in the Midwest or Rust Belt (a term we use with affection), we understand that the various forms of oppression and marginalization that we struggle against are not the sum total of our existence. Just as we have known pain and suffering and struggle, we have known joy and love and care. So we fight—because we know that we are worth fighting for.

We stand in solidary with numerous other organizations, collectives, and movements that are committed to the cause of freedom and social justice for black people and other minoritized populations, both in the U.S. and abroad. We see our work as but a small part of a much larger push toward liberation that neither begins nor ends with us, but which we are uniquely situated to contribute to. We welcome anyone who is similarly committed to join with us.

Find out more at theblackmidwest.com

Contents

I. HOME

II. PAST

Contents

V. ONWARD

Contents

END NOTES

Foreword: The Rise of the Fresh Coast

JAMALA ROGERS

In October 2019, I was a presenter at the inaugural Black Midwest Symposium, which was titled "Black in the Middle" and hosted by the Black Midwest Initiative at the University of Minnesota, Twin Cities. I shared the program booklet with a twenty-something when I got back to St. Louis. She looked slowly at the couple dozen headshots of participants on the front page.

"I don't recognize any of these people." There was almost a tinge of guilt in her voice.

That's exactly the point. No national superstars. Just Black people in the Midwest doing their things in their own remarkable ways.

The symposium brought together writers, students, artists, scholars, organizers, and others to build community and celebrate our unsung contributions to the cultural, political, and economic fabric of the Black Liberation Movement.

It was not ironic that the first gathering would be held in the state where the term "Minnesota Nice" has come to identify its residents. The mythology suggests that those who live in the state are mild-mannered, reserved, and non-confrontational.

Some years ago, Matt Nelson coined the phrase "Fresh Coast." Nelson was an organizer in Milwaukee at the time. The clever expression was his way of elevating the Midwest as an equal to the overshadowing coasts of the East and West. Just without the oceans.

Like a middle child, Black Midwesterners have struggled to project our unique identity, sandwiched between two pretentious sibling coasts. Our collective mannerism often comes across as subdued and unassuming. The history contradicts that myth on so many levels.

The modest posture means that our contributions are often eclipsed by the dazzle of the coasts. The "Black in the Middle" symposium amplified the genius of those of African descent situated throughout the Midwest and Rust Belt regions. We exist in mostly Red states under the Republican rule and all it heaps on us. Yet still we rise.

The driving goal of the symposium was to create a space where we could share how our Midwestern grounding affects our unapologetic Black lives and worldviews. It bolstered the mutual affirmation and collective knowledge of our accomplishments across several sectors—cultural, electoral, academic, housing, and labor.

The symposium panels explored old concepts—space, freedom and justice—in new and creative ways. Extraordinary thinkers and determined catalysts examined these topics using a lens of imagination rooted in the complexities of the region and the country.

The rousing success of the first symposium justifies a second gathering. It was clear that participants made impacts wherever we planted our feet and raised our fists. We will have to step up our game in the current period of anti-Blackness and racialized capitalism. In this next period, I urge us to think about how we will create and strengthen the kind of Black organizations necessary for the challenges we will face.

A weakened Black Left in the U.S. has impacted our capacity to make a serious, collective political analysis and bold strategic moves that register us on the power scale. The Black Liberation Movement has the talent and skills but we must learn from the past lessons of our history. Our brilliance is being overshadowed by mediocrity and disunity. Our people need effective organizations and formidable institutions that can build upon our political, cultural, and economic legacies. We must be committed to nurturing the kind of Blackness based upon common liberatory values and goals.

In a series of articles for the BlackCommentator.com titled "Unblocking Our Movement Chakras," I tapped into my decades of organizing along with the wisdom of other organizers and those being organized. I identified what I believe are our key internal obstacles choking our spirit and progress.

In a capitalist world that praises individualism and biases of all descriptions, even politically conscious people are not exempt from being lulled into the world of I'm-so-smart-I-don't-need-anybody-else. Individualism and liberalism run rampant in our collective spaces. This allows a few people to hold hostage our efforts to move strategic goals forward in a cohesive manner. The undesirable result is needless conflict, demoralization, and stagnation.

In 2020, the Black Midwest could be the beacon for the rest of the country. Let's sharpen our analyses and re-commit to a vision of real liberation. Let's be intentional about building and fortifying our movement by embracing a humane strategy that recognizes the savagery of capitalism. Let's raise the bar of accountability—to be genuine in our self-criticism and more loving in our constructive criticism of other freedom fighters. Let's root out unhealthy practices in our personal and political lives that undermine our unity and our humanity.

My Midwest Brothers and Sisters, we can do this. Let the nation know the Fresh Coast is rising.

This Place We Know: An Introduction

Each year since at least 2015, the online financial news site *24/7 Wall St.* has published a list it calls the "Worst Cities for Black Americans." The list, which is determined by way of an index that is culled largely from Census data, is based on socioeconomic disparities between black and white residents according to eight different measures, including homeownership, educational attainment, unemployment rates, household income, and rates of incarceration. If you haven't seen this now-infamous list, perhaps the news won't surprise you. Or maybe it will. Of the fifteen cities and metro areas named in the most recent 2019 edition of the list, fourteen are located within the Midwest and larger industrial sector of the U.S. (i.e., the Rust Belt). As ever, my own hometown of Peoria, Illinois made the list, as did the hometown of my grandmother and mother, Danville, Illinois, a city with a population of about 33,000 that is located 120 miles east of Peoria on I-74.

The Twin Cities—Minneapolis and St. Paul—where the Black Midwest Initiative is based and where the symposium that occasioned this volume was held in October 2019, makes an appearance on the list as well. Although the poverty rate for white residents in the Twin Cities is well below the national poverty rate, the poverty rate for black residents is well above it. High rates of residential segregation and disparities in home ownership birthed out of a long history of restrictive housing covenants and exclusionary zoning policies are among the factors that helped the Twin Cities earn their place on the "worst of" list. This placement is quite the twist given that the Twin Cities, unlike many of the other cities on the list, are regularly named among the best places to live in the country. In fact, in 2019, the same year that the Twin Cities landed fourth on the list of worst cities for black Americans, they landed sixth on *U.S. News & World Report's* list of the "125 Best Places to Live in the USA." Black life is nothing if not ironic.

While Minneapolis, St. Paul, Peoria, and Danville are cities of dramatically different size and character (because it turns out that every place in the Midwest isn't actually the same) what they share in common with each other, with each of the cities on the *24/7* list, and with a whole host of Midwestern cities that didn't make the list besides, is that the conditions under which black people live are, and historically have been, in stark contrast to the experiences of many other residents of those same cities. You might argue, pretty credibly in fact, that there is nothing particularly particular to the Midwest in this—that black life is conditioned by precarity wherever it is lived. But what is distinct about black Midwesterners is the extent to which our lives fail to register collectively as worthy of sustained attention except, of course, in moments of crisis when the national spotlight hones in just long enough to use us as fodder for the expediencies of political outrage—think Chicago, Flint, Detroit, Ferguson. Even as electoral campaign cycles mobilize, rhetorically if not in fact, around the plight of heartland laborers, the disproportionate and specific consequences of deindustrialization, population loss, and economic decline on black Midwestern communities remains conspicuously unaddressed.

Black in the Middle attests to the fact that lists such as those named above, however wrong or right they are, can only tell a very small part of the story. Those of us who have spent our lives in the Midwest don't need business models or economic data to tell us what we have lived— what our bodies have felt, what our eyes have seen. Even those among us who don't have a bunch of degrees or fancy academic jargon or professional training at our disposal understand the maneuverings of racialized disinvestment and dispossession. We have intimate experience with social upheaval and crumbling infrastructure and impoverished educational systems and housing insecurity and targeted police brutality and poisoned water and morally and financially bankrupt governments and serialized black death and municipal plunder and manufacturing malaise and climate catastrophe and queer-bashing, Muslim-hating, racist-sexist so-and-sos who aren't actually any of those things, they just want to make America great again. As the brilliant poet and activist Sunni Patterson once so eloquently put it in reference to her beloved New Orleans, "we know this place."

But, speaking of brilliance, there is yet another roll call we black Midwesterners know something about, and it goes a little something like this: Gwendolyn Brooks. Richard Pryor. Malcolm X. Fred Hampton. Earvin "Magic" Johnson. Miles Davis. The Obamas. Gordon Parks. Oscar Micheaux. Kanye West ('cause like your ruinous second cousin who you avoid like the plague until the family reunion, you have to claim him—and fight for him too). Quincy Jones. Langston

Hughes. Diana Ross. Karen Lewis. Prince. Charlie Parker. Janet Jackson (and them). Aretha Franklin. Rita Dove. The Clark Sisters. Dorothy Dandridge. LeBron James. Maya Angelou. Bootsy Collins. Lizzo. Toni Morrison. Stepping in Chicago. Funk in Dayton. Motown in— Motown. Perhaps you. Certainly me. You get the point. This is to say that for all that has, and continues to, plague us, the Midwest has also birthed and helped to mold some of the most significant, innovate, and consequential thinkers and cultural producers in American history, black or otherwise—to say nothing of the scores of unheralded community organizers, homegrown intellectuals, artists, writers, and other creatives, teachers, spiritual advisors, and neighborhood folks who do the work of building us up and holding us down every single day. We do indeed know this place.

When we gathered together at the University of Minnesota last October for what the Initiative called "Black in the Middle: The Inaugural Black Midwest Symposium," we came together in a spirit of sharing and openness to think through the meaning of black life in the middle—not just the geographic middle, but also black life in the middle of any number of social and political cataclysms that we were, and are, struggling against individually and collectively. We explored and made explicit our frustrations, but we also shared our success stories and strategies for getting through and pushing forward. This book is an extension of the critical work we began there. While not all of the contributors to this volume were present at the symposium and not all of the presenters at the symposium made contributions to this volume, the work of each endeavor speaks to the other and is part of a collective project to make visible the struggle and the agony, yes, but also the diversity and richness of black Midwestern life.

One of the most important missions of the Black Midwest Initiative is to bring together people from across a range of creative, intellectual, and professional fields, and that mission is born out within the pages of this book. The forty-plus contributors to *Black in the Middle* are visual artists and poets, teachers and students, organizers and scholars, performance artists and filmmakers. Our training is both formal and informal. Some of us work in institutions and with organizations, while others of us work in the streets or out of our homes—many of us do some combination of all of the above. We come from cities big and small, and places urban and rural. Many of us still call the Midwest home, while others of us have moved on to different (notice that I did not say *greener*) pastures. We also have a wide range of viewpoints and divergent points of entry into the issues that matter to us most. What we share in common, however, is the desire to expand the discussion of the Midwest beyond narrow political talking points and misinformed media portrayals and to share with you, the reader, our individual yet deeply connected experiences of this place we know.

Terrion L. Williamson
February 2020
Minneapolis, Minnesota

Ode to the Midwest

KEVIN YOUNG

The country I come from
Is called the Midwest
—Bob Dylan

I want to be doused
in cheese

& fried. I want
to wander

the aisles, my heart's
supermarket stocked high

as cholesterol. I want to die
wearing a sweatsuit—

I want to live
forever in a Christmas sweater,

a teddy bear nursing
off the front. I want to write

a check in the express lane.
I want to scrape

my driveway clean

myself, early, before
anyone's awake—

that'll put em to shame—
I want to see what the sun

sees before it tells
the snow to go. I want to be

the only black person I know.

I want to throw
out my back & not

complain about it.
I wanta drive

two blocks. Why walk—

I want to love, n stuff—

I want to cut
my sutures myself.

I want to jog
down to the river

& make it my bed—

I want to walk
its muddy banks

& make me a withdrawal.

I tried jumping in,
found it frozen—

I'll go home, I guess,
to my rooms where the moon

changes & shines
like television.

I.
HOME

For one's language, the one we dream in, is home.
—Toni Morrison

(Born in Lorain, Ohio, 1931)

Rust: A Black Woman's Story of Growing Up in Northeast Ohio

TARA L. CONLEY

I only know weathered women. Women like my great-grandmother who stared at the lines on her palm to predict a change in the air. Like my aunt, an exercise instructor who ran away to Chicago only to return home with a stroke. And my grandmother, who left one morning in her burgundy Pontiac. She died three months later, after the car accident. My mom withered down to 90 pounds while taking care of my grandmother when she was in a coma. I lost my memory.

For the women I know, shouldering the burden of unemployment, drug addiction, and family dysfunction comes at a high price. Some were abused. Many died. Some loved thick, but that kind of love was never returned. Others left for a short time and came back, maybe because of shame or guilt or maybe because Northeast Ohio was all they really knew.

In places like Northeast Ohio, where it seems only working-class White Trump voters exist, Black women are living in racially segregated neighborhoods, and their babies are dying at alarming rates, all while leading the fight against corrupt law enforcement agencies. Though some studies give us a sense of the social and environmental stressors Black women confront in the Rust Belt, more often than not, statistics aren't disaggregated by gender and race, making it even more pressing that Black women's stories from the Midwest are told.

In this region of the country, home is possessive. And the choice to leave, when presented, is rarely an easy one. You either leave Northeast Ohio for better opportunities, or you stay to build a life. This choice is especially salient for Black families. Despite social conditions that have plagued the lives of poor and low-income Black Americans, there's still a shared sense of struggle and history that makes this place we call home ours.

In Elyria, Ohio, the small town where I grew up, racial segregation has been a defining characteristic since its inception in 1817 when European settlers occupied Native American territory. According to The Housing Center, the Cleveland-Elyria metropolitan area is the fifth-most racially segregated region in the United States. Poverty statistics for Cuyahoga and Lorain counties rate above pre-recession levels at 33% and 15% respectively. When Black people are lucky enough to own property in this region, home values in Black neighborhoods tend to decrease. But when Black people buy homes in predominantly White neighborhoods, values tend to increase because, as historian Richard Rothstein notes in his book *The Color of Law: A Forgotten History of How Our Government Segregated America*, Black people are willing to pay more for homes in White neighborhoods due to housing supply restrictions in predominantly Black neighborhoods.

In 2012, the *New York Times* profiled Elyria with an interactive piece called "This Land" by Dan Berry. It features a story about Ike Maxwell, a former Elyria High School football star whose life went awry after his 19-year-old brother was shot and killed by a White Elyria police officer. Over the several years that followed, Ike suffered multiple physical injuries, mental illness, and drug abuse. He was collateral damage in a racially divided town.

My mom grew up with Ike. She gets angry anytime we talk about his story. Perhaps she felt some responsibility to Ike, like most Black women do to the men and boys we know. Perhaps she was angry because the town she grew up in failed Ike, and outsiders could see why. My mom doesn't much care for the *Times'* profile of Elyria. To her, the Times version of the land isn't her home.

Stories coming from mainstream press about Black and White life in the Midwest often get distorted. Decades of industrial decline and the war on drugs helped shape these narratives. But drug addiction didn't start when Donald Trump was elected; neither did White economic anxiety. The economic downturn in Northeast Ohio began decades ago when steel and automotive industries left town. Family members struggled with mental illness and drug addiction long before these were considered national crises, and a scarcity of local resources and unemployment had a lot to do with it. It's true that Black and White families suffered. Though, in comparison, Black families were less likely than White families to recover from economic decline and high unemployment. When White people managed, Black folks endured.

Over time, Rust Belt neighborhoods like Elyria appeared stuck in a Norman Rockwell painting, except buildings that were once quintessential landmarks of an idyllic, bustling town became dilapidated and abandoned. In this world, there is no burgeoning middle class, and Black people aren't seen in the foreground of American life. This vignette appears in American politics too. Despite the fact that two of the largest counties in Northeast Ohio, Cuyahoga and Lorain, voted for Hillary Clinton in 2016, many of them Black voters, Whites who voted for Trump remain the sole face of the Midwest working class in Northeast Ohio.

And perhaps for this reason, as a way to feel unstuck and write my own story, I left Northeast Ohio after high school.

I am a child of the Loving Generation. My experience of class in Northeast Ohio was greatly influenced by my father's racial privilege and my mother's blue-collar work ethic. Growing up in a working-class family meant financial stability was temporary. My parents had good jobs that didn't last. They were pro-union. They were also an interracial couple in a newly desegregated world. They were firsts. My mom was the first Black female lineman for the Elyria Telephone Company in the 1970s, and my dad, a White superintendent at General Motors, advocated for Black workers to organize and receive fair treatment in the workplace. They married in 1979, 18 years after the Supreme Court decision *Loving v. Virginia* overturned laws outlawing interracial marriage in the U.S. Though their marriage was legal, our family still had to navigate overt racial discrimination in Northeast Ohio.

Though they didn't know it at the time, my parents engaged in a tactic that early civil rights groups used to bring attention to racial discrimination in housing. My dad was the family's tester. He scouted rental properties around town because my parents had a better chance of renting a place if the landlord knew a White man was signing the lease, not a Black mother. My experience, although not the norm, underscores the psychological harm families endure when Black women aren't valued.

Often in our imaginings of life in the Heartland, we forget that Black women have, for decades, sustained social institutions as the economy around them decayed. Their stories go unnoticed, perhaps because it's easier to ignore the gradual process of systematic brokenness than to confront it.

But these stories must be told in order to make right what Anne Trubek calls "narrative inequality." Because when statistics about economic anxiety, voter suppression, and health epidemics in the Midwest dominate the national news, we'll remember that Black women have been embattled with these conditions for generations. We'll avoid using stories as a means of speculating about a panacea for the economic anxieties of White voters. We'll recognize that Black life in the Midwest has always existed despite the single story of Whiteness.

We'll remember that none of this is new.

Then we can ask better questions, like how do we slow down the process of weathering women? Although decades of Black women sustaining social institutions to the detriment of their health can't be reversed, it is possible to reduce further harm by addressing the systemic disregard of Black life that causes Black women to suffer in the first place. It requires paying attention to the health and well-being of Black women and mothers and organizing at the local level to end racial and gender discrimination in housing, law enforcement, schools, and in the workforce. While there appear to be signs of hope for legislation supporting maternal health care for Black women that would help Black women in my hometown, a seismic shift in policy priorities to address issues affecting Black women is still necessary.

And perhaps telling Black women's stories can set this shift in motion. Because when our stories are told, something happens: Weathering slows down. And the burden of maintaining a normal life amid broken communities will no longer fall on the shoulders of the women we know.

This essay was originally published online on October 29, 2019 for ZORA, a Medium publication for women of color.

References

Berry, Dan. "This Land." *The New York Times*, October 14, 2012.
https://archive.nytimes.com/www.nytimes.com/
interactive/2012/10/14/us/this-land-elyria-ohio.html

Rothstein, Richard. *The Color of Law: A Forgotten History of How Our Government Segregated America.* New York: Liverlight Publishing Corporation, 2017.

Trubek, Anne. *Voices from the Rust Belt*. New York: Picador, 2018

Lepley, Michael and Lenore Magiarelli, *The State of Fair Housing in Northeast Ohio* (The Housing Center: Housing Research and Advocacy Center, 2017). http://www.thehousingcenter.org/wp-content/uploads/2017/04/SOFH-2017-Final.pdf 2017

There Are Birds Here

JAMAAL MAY

There are birds here,
so many birds here
is what I was trying to say
when they said those birds were metaphors
for what is trapped
between buildings
and buildings. No.
The birds are here
to root around for bread
the girl's hands tear
and toss like confetti. No,
I don't mean the bread is torn like cotton,
I said confetti, and no
not the confetti
a tank can make of a building.
I mean the confetti
a boy can't stop smiling about
and no his smile isn't much
like a skeleton at all. And no
his neighborhood is not like a warzone.
I am trying to say
his neighborhood
is as tattered and feathered
as anything else,
as shadow pierced by sun
and light parted
by shadow-dance as anything else,
but they won't stop saying
how lovely the ruins,
how ruined the lovely
children must be in that birdless city.

This poem appears in The Big Book of Exit Strategies *(Alice James Books, 2016).*

Hood Orchids

DEVON GINN

on the side of my childhood
home, a bushel of tiger lilies
bloomed absurd, bold

between a rusted chain-link
fence and a rubber
hose beveled from its

harmony with the wire.
my mother called them
orchids—I would

use the kitchen shears
my family cut our
oven-ready-pizza with

to decapitate a dozen
'hood orchids at an angle
as I was once directed.

I placed this batch in a large
fast food cup filled with water
from the hose—my gift to her

she took beige twine—wrapped
it around the plastic—sprinkled
blue sugar between the leaves—

sat them on a
 sunlit shelf,
  and taught
   me to find
    the beauty in
     collaboration

Gentrification and the South Side of Ypsilanti, Michigan

AARON K. FOLEY

The center of Ypsilanti has what we call the Brick Dick. It is an unfortunately phallic-shaped water tower with a dark dome at the top and a lighter base beneath, making it look like a stone-grey erect penis right smack-dab in the middle of town. In my lifetime, I've never known the Ypsilanti Water Tower, the site's official name, to hold water. But I can tell you that this thousand-ton dildo isn't even the weirdest thing about Ypsilanti, Michigan.

There is a liquor store on the edge of town—that's what the rest of you might call a "corner store" or "bodega," or sometimes a "party store"—that no one really calls by its name, even though its real name, which you can Google by searching "Ypsilanti cow" is Carry Dairy, and it has a giant steer on its roof. There's the motel at the split near Prospect and Ecorse roads, where my mother's friend raves about the prostitutes who stand outside completely nude and smoking cigarettes between johns. There's the purported "man with no face," who presumably suffered some sort of awful accident but never got it properly treated, and he can be seen in and around the campus of Eastern Michigan University, which is right next to the Brick Dick. There was once a serial pooper who defecated in parks across Ypsi.

Look past your usual small-town shenanigans and scandals, and this is a place where everybody knows everybody's business. My cousin played football, and now he's a football coach. His sister was a cheerleader, now she coaches cheerleading, and her son played in the little league where her brother coaches. And they gossip about the parents (once their classmates) and their kids just like my aunt, their mom, gossips about the now-grandparents in her generation, the children of the parents in my grandparents' circle. And my grandparents keep abreast with the latest in Ypsilanti through volunteering at the church, nights at the VFW, funerals at Lucille's, and casual run-ins at one of two town squares: the Walmart on Ellsworth Road, or Facebook. Ypsilanti is where black folks came up south to stay—and never left. I joke that Ypsilanti is a town from Kentucky that got lost in Michigan. (And there's merit to that; most of the white people that first came here did indeed come from Kentucky, and the nickname—for better or worse—of "Ypsitucky" started to stick.) It feels worlds away from Detroit, the hyper-industrial Motor City that's only a 40-minute drive east. It feels just as distant from Ann Arbor, the famously liberal home of the University of Michigan, only six miles away, only separated by bland Pittsfield Township.

Like a lot of places in the north, black people came to Ypsilanti for two reasons: First, to escape slavery, and then later to work in plants. And when I say "they never left," it's because Ypsi didn't have the black exodus to the suburbs like other major cities—Detroit included—did. Black roots run so far deep here, it's not uncommon for singles to double-check to make sure they're not related, either by blood or by marriage, to potential romantic partners because of relationships, legitimate or otherwise, that happened generations ago. Or maybe just one generation ago.

Sometimes I tell people that Ypsilanti is the only place where the hood, the cornfields, the suburbs, the country club, and the college town are all in one city, and if you drive five miles in any direction from the center of town, you'll never know which one you'll run into first. A lot of the roads in the newer subdivisions were still dirt up until my early 1990s childhood. Conversely, the streets were paved on the South Side because the elite women of the Palm Leaf Club, an age-old black women's social club, demanded city action because they didn't want their dresses to get dusty as they walked to church. And redlining explains why West Willow, the other black side of town, became West Willow; black Ypsilantians weren't allowed to live in close proximity to the Willow Run Bomber Plant, so they were herded out west.

My family weaves in and out of all these narratives of Ypsilanti. My mother's degree-holding parents moved up the career ladder and further out from the west side of Detroit and found themselves in one of the then-newer subdivisions of Ypsilanti in the early 1970s. Her dad, my grandfather, ran the juvenile facility at the psychiatric hospital there, the old Ypsilanti State Hospital. My mother came of age in Ypsi, bowling at the Ypsi-Arbor Bowl and watching blaxploitation flicks at Wayside Theater. (Both have been torn down.) And she met my father at Ypsi High. His dad, my other grandfather, used to work at the Ford plant on the outskirts of Ypsi before becoming a detective with the police force. They were from one Foley family on the South Side, on Ainsworth Circle. The other Foley family on the South Side, and also on Ainsworth Circle, were also related to them, but there was enough separation on the family tree down the years that they were considered two different families, for whatever reason.

Beyond its quirks and oddities, its complicated past, its various identities, black folks hold strong in Ypsilanti. My parents divorced and my mother raised me in Detroit, but after years of being away, she ended up moving back to Ypsilanti—and not the subdivision where her parents were, but the South Side. On Ainsworth Circle, less than a five-minute walk from her former in-laws. And I remember her neighbor, a widowed black man, telling me, "this is a place where black folks can take pride in living."

Go all up and through South Side Ypsi, where slaves who found freedom first came in the 1800s, and built the first black church, Brown Chapel A.M.E., in 1843, and you'll see the lilies and rosebushes on the borders of manicured lawns, the driveways with Ford vehicles (because that X-Plan for relatives of retirees won't ever go away here), and little black grands and great-grands playing in the yards—especially on Ainsworth Circle. And then maybe you'll also see a young white couple walking their dog and shitting on someone else's lawn.

It's the "little dogs shitting all over these people's yards" that drive my uncle, who lives on the South Side, on Ainsworth Circle, insane. "I had to get on them," he said, and let them know that they don't tolerate that here on the Circle.

For as long as I've been alive, the Ypsilanti I'm most familiar with has been comfortably integrated. Three interracial couples—one family in the house on the left, another family in the house on the right that was succeeded by another one—lived next door to the house my mom's parents lived in. One was a white woman and black man, whose kids I used to play with every summer. Another was a black woman and a white man. And another was a Swede and an East Asian woman, whose son had hair redder and curlier than Raggedy Andy. Eastern Michigan University attracted black students from Detroit, and white students from all over the place. Indian residents who came to work white-collar jobs in the automotive industry or study at the University of Michigan lived there too. Across the street from my mom's parents' house was a true Ypsituckian, a gun-toting white woman who had a Doberman, several male lovers, and an accent like Tanya Tucker. She, my grandmother, and another white woman next door to her whose husband retired from Ford, smoked cigarettes with each other in their respective living rooms and made each other meals.

On the South Side where my dad's parents were, it was and still is like how my mom's now-neighbor describes: Where black folks can take pride in living. They didn't have to go to a separate school; Ypsi's schools were integrated. They didn't have to go to separate stores; Briarwood Mall in Ann Arbor was open to all. And it's not like the South Side black folks didn't mingle with the black folks in the country, the subdivisions or near the country club, because at the end of the day, black was black. Black Ypsilantians owned the South Side because there was pride in black ownership.

So where did the white people with shitting dogs come from?

That's what everyone on the South Side has been asking for the past few years. Why do y'all want to come here now? The answer can be found in a few national trends.

The South Side is just a hop, skip and a jump from downtown Ypsilanti, which has all the character of any small town's downtown that came up in the Industrial Age, but now has craft beer. That makes it, as real estate agents might say, "walkable." There's walkability from the South Side to craft beer.

Then there are the homes themselves. All that pride in ownership over the last few decades, coming from folks like my dad's father who has worked with his hands all his life, meant these homes—of course, the ones that date back to the 1800s where aforementioned freed slaves once lived, but a bunch of which also fall into another buzzy trend, "midcentury"—have been kept up. That means no tough rehab projects for any potential buyers.

But overall, it's the cost of living. Millennials can't afford to buy a house—unless they buy a house in South Side Ypsilanti. And you know Ann Arbor, home to that world-renowned university which attracts interest from around the world, which is now building more and more high-rises to accommodate demand, which has craft beer pouring out from every bistro and osteria and gastropub on every block, whose unabashed white liberalism comes at an extreme cost? People are fleeing Ann Arbor to the other college town next door, and they're bringing their discerning tastes—and shitting dogs—with them.

Gentrification is starting to rear its ugly head in the one place in Southeast Michigan I thought it would never come. When gentrification is discussed in Southeast Michigan, all eyes are usually on Detroit, which is where I grew up and is undergoing its fifth or sixth renaissance, rebound, rebirth, whatever you might want to call it, since I've been alive. Except it seems for real this time, because after decades of white flight from Detroit, white people are buying homes left and right in the hood, and you know when the white people come back, it means a city is on the rise. Here's the thing, though: Detroit is so damn big and empty, it would take forever for any other class beyond the middle- and working-class black folks that make up almost 80 percent of the place to make them budge.

Ypsilanti is different. It is not vacant, it is not large, and it is ripe for the kind of gentrification seen in places like Austin, where an influx of discerning white folks with money could easily erase the black parts of the city's culture. Or San Francisco, where white folks call the cops on the neighbors that have been there all this time. They're not artists coming in first, followed by the gay couples and young degree-holders. They're likely Ann Arbor ex-pats who'd put those "you are welcome here" signs in their front yard and not actually welcome anyone if they'd shown up on their doorstep.

At first when my uncle raised these concerns, I tried to talk him down. I said that just because you have new white neighbors, it doesn't mean they're going to build a Whole Foods next week. (And to be clear, Ypsi doesn't need one. There's a lovely food co-op outside of Depot Town, a historic district straddling a railroad, and a regular farmers' market.) But then the textbook examples of gentrification quickly started to show. People started knocking on doors on the South Side asking if they'd consider selling their homes. More "Ann Arbor-esque" businesses started opening downtown. Rent prices started going up. Real estate comps started going up and when a house went for sale, the sale price would always be higher than asking, and whoever bought it probably wasn't black.

Whispers of gentrification reached the press in Detroit, but reporters only asked longtime white residents what they thought. No one queried blacks on the South Side, so Facebook—again, Ypsi's town square—became the information channel for them to vent. My uncle organized panel discussions at Parkridge Community Center, the South Side's rec center that the neighborhood had to lobby the city government for increased funding, and announced them on Facebook in all caps: GENTRIFICA-TION: THE CHANGING FACES OF YPSILANTI'S SOUTH SIDE and GENTRIFICATION, ECONOMICS AND SYSTEMIC RACISM PT. 2. Candidates running for office started paying more attention to the voices from the South Side. And perhaps the biggest strike against gentrification was when the entire community rallied against a potential new development that seemed to have good intention—it was a housing complex designed for international students attending the colleges in the area—that for sure would have jacked up housing prices if approved. (Turns out, the Chinese developer wanting to build might have bribed Ypsilanti housing officials with a free trip to China to get them on board with the plan. Maybe. It hasn't been proven yet.)

But I wonder if Facebook and meetings are enough to keep the South

Side's character intact. I'd like to see it continue as "the place where black folks can take pride in living." I'd also like to see more conversation around towns and suburbs where black folks have made their home for generations possibly losing ground to market forces and ever-changing tastes of the upwardly mobile. Don't black folks deserve that brand of small-town, folksy lifestyle we've seen white folks have in the movies and episodic dramas for years? Like damn, can't we have anything? That's what I want for Ypsilanti, for us to keep what little we have.

Traveling While Black

TANISHA C. FORD

I was somewhere between asleep and awake. It was Christmas Eve, 1987, and we were cruising up Indiana State Highway 37 in my mom's 1973 Ford Mustang—cobalt blue—making the trek from Bloomington, Indiana to our hometown of Fort Wayne, so we could celebrate Christmas with family. The sounds of Walter Hawkins's *Love Alive II*, a tape mom kept in steady rotation, were blaring through the car's speakers.

Over Hawkins's "Be Grateful," I could hear my mom, in the driver's seat, bickering with my aunt, who was riding shotgun. My eight-year-old spirit registered a panic in my aunt's voice that I had never heard from her before. "Girl, we can't stop! We're in Martinsville," my aunt said.

Mom firmly told her that we *had* to stop because the car's headlights were out. I looked out the window, which was still slightly iced over. Darkness had chased us down, leaving nothing but a midnight blue mass of sky. In front of the Mustang, where long cylinders of white light should have been emanating to guide us up the highway, there was only black. But my aunt was willing to risk the possibility of sliding off the slick, winding road, rather than stop in Martinsville, Indiana.

I was too young to know it then, but this was the cause of the panic: we were a car of two Black women and a Black girl in a reputed sundown town of southern Indiana—after dark.

Sundown towns are communities that have historically been "all white on purpose," their whiteness enforced either officially (in the past, some towns had signs posted with messages like "Whites Only Within City Limits After Dark") or through unofficial, often violent means. Thousands of sundown towns existed across the country. By some estimates, there were as many as two hundred in Indiana alone. And they are not unique to small towns—James Loewen, in his book *Sundown Towns: A Hidden Dimension of American Racism*, identifies "sundown suburbs" of larger cities. Many sundown towns remain overwhelmingly, if not exclusively, white.

News of Black folks being threatened, beaten, and lynched in places like these spread rapidly through our communities' informal networks. Some of those stories had been circulating since the 1920s and '30s, when there was a resurgence in Klan activity in Indiana and across the U.S. Black women were particularly vulnerable to beatings and lynchings, as well as sexual assaults. It's what prompted the publication of *The Negro Motorist Green Book* in 1936 (which was published regularly until 1966). The only people who have the luxury of ignoring this history are those who haven't had to order their lives by that unofficial rule and the vigilante violence that was promised if you were caught in a sundown town at dusk.

Beyond its reputation as a sundown town, Martinsville was also known as the epicenter of Klan terror in Indiana. I had never heard of Martinsville before, but I was intrigued by this infamous place that could reduce a grown woman to near tears. I jolted up in my seat, butting into the conversation. "What's Martinsville? What's wrong with the car? What are you scared of, Aunt Janice? Are we gonna make it home in time to open my Christmas gifts?"

No one in our car uttered the words "sundown town"; that was a language I'd come to know later in life. For now, I was getting a particular kind of geography lesson. I didn't know where Martinsville was on a map in relationship to Fort Wayne, but I was learning that I wasn't supposed to be there. I added it to a list that included Waynedale and Huntington, places I'd also heard the adults in my life say to stay clear of. Conversely, in Indianapolis, we could find communities of people who looked like us, soul food restaurants, concerts, and big events like the Circle City Classic, which catered to Black folks.

The lesson was clear: navigating the state was less about knowing direction and more about knowing "your place." Mom and Aunt Janice seemed to know—instinctively, it seemed—where they belonged and where they didn't. And clearly, Martinsville was the latter.

☙

We pulled into a mom and pop gas station. A string of Christmas lights framed the shop window. The clerk on duty, an older white man, peeked his head out. Seeing our dark bodies emerging from the car, he walked outside, slowly, with a perplexed look on his face. Presumably, because Black folks knew to steer clear of Martinsville, whites in Martinsville had become accustomed to rarely, if ever, seeing us in real life.

My mother explained what had brought us to his establishment on this crisp winter evening. I searched the man's eyes for some telltale sign of his comfort level. He wasn't outwardly hostile—I'd experienced overt racism enough times in my young life to know what it looked like. But he also wasn't kind in that way that mom and dad's white friends who came to the house were.

Mom and the clerk performed an awkward dance of human politeness as he led us into the gas station so mom could call my father collect. He offered us space to sit inside while we waited for my father to arrive. Aunt Janice was fixing her mouth to say "hell no!" when my mother jumped in and politely declined his offer, saying we would wait in the car. Mom and Aunt Janice poured cups of the shop's bitter coffee to help them stay alert. We made our way back to the car.

No one bothered us. Not even the clerk, who had returned to his mundane shop duties. But my mother and aunt began sharing stories with me—some joyous, some utterly terrifying—about what is was like to be college students in Klan country during the peak years of the Black Power movement.

In 1968, just four years before my mother arrived on IU's campus, a twenty-one-year-old Black encyclopedia saleswoman named Carol Jenkins was brutally murdered in Martinsville by a Klan member. The murder went unsolved for more than three decades. Meanwhile, hundreds of young Black women like my mother left their homes each year to attend IU, the specter of Jenkins' murder a constant reminder that they could never—and would never—feel or be safe.

The racial violence of the area was even more explicit for my family. My mom told me her brother, my uncle Howard, was beaten bloody in Martinsville when he, not being from the area, stopped to get food on his way to visit her at college.

The IU campus wasn't even a refuge from anti-Black harassment. My mom told stories of the KKK marching on public streets. University police officers would harass Black students for gathering on the yard in groups considered "too large." White professors assumed that Black students were not prepared for the rigors of college, often grading them more harshly than their white counterparts. Many of these stories of racial discrimination on campus were chronicled in the IU Arbutus yearbook, given titles such as "Black Life in the Ivory Tower." These stories mirrored those written on the pages of *Essence* in the early '70s, by and about Black students at predominantly white institutions.

Up until that Christmas Eve, the only depictions I'd seen of the Klan were in films, like the scene in *Lady Sings the Blues* (1972), in which Klan members attack Billie Holiday's tour bus, hitting her in the eye with the butt of a wooden stake. But here I was, now, hearing of my own family's encounters with these enigmas in white hoods. I now understood that there were fleshy bodies underneath those hoods—real people—who hated us simply because we were Black.

℘

But in the quiet spaces of their dorm rooms and apartments, mom and her peers could dance out their rage, they could style out their rage. I could hear it in their voices, in the ways they told their stories, but it would not truly sink in until I was much older: survival then—as it is now—was about stealing moments of intoxicating pleasure amidst many more that were singed by violence.

I heard tales of Black, sweaty bodies doing dances like "the dawg" and "the hustle" at the annual Omega Psi Phi *Mardi Gras* party. Mom and her friends would go decked out in elephant-leg pants—bout the widest bell bottoms you'll ever see—and lace-front dresses and knee-high boots, with their Afros picked just so. Those parties were safe havens where young Black folks, who were few in number on campus, could dance and listen to soul and funk tracks—unapologetically young and Black.

My mom and my aunt had gotten into a rhythm, telling their stories, feeding off of each other like a well-trained performance duo. Black girl hand gestures abounded. Aunt Janice would let out her signature screeching cackle when things got really funny. Mom's voice would boom when she told one of her "bet not no one mess with me" stories. They laughed as they tried to remember the name of "so-and-so's boyfriend" who did "woopty woop" at "such-and-such's" apartment "that one night." I learned of the men my mom loved long before she and my father became a thing.

I would interject here and there with questions, wanting more details to add to the mental movie of the past that I was directing in my head. But for the most part, I knew to keep quiet because something big, something important was happening here. This was more than a mere passing of the time. This was two Black women trying to work through fear and trauma, sharing their vulnerability with me, a girl of a different era, of a different generation, but of the same blood. Through them, I experienced the full range of Black emotion, their stories offering a context for my aunt's fear earlier that evening. It came from a real place.

By the time my father dashed up to the gas station in his big, mint green Mercury Cougar to rescue his wife and daughter, I felt a little older, a little less innocent. I had come face-to-face with white supremacy, learning at a young age that people will do anything—including taking a life—in order to maintain some semblance of power. It was a rite of passage that, even then, I knew my white peers did not have to experience. Their privilege shielded them from ever having to learn about this real American horror story. Yet, the trauma of the past was now etched into my skin. To be a Black girl in this world meant pain would be part of the experience.

But my passage also taught me about Black resilience, Black joy, Black creativity. Something about sharing the tiny space of the old Mustang with my mom and my aunt helped us to bond. For those few hours, we were on equal footing. All of us scared, and them telling stories to keep the haints away. The stories were our survival. The air never went silent.

The Market on Maryland Avenue

TERRENCE SHAMBLEY JR.

took down the balloon and bottle memorial tucked in the corner of their parking lot for the boy shot dead there not even a month ago. Me and my mom are on our way home from walking around the lake, and I tell her I'ma buy that store one day, and the gas station up the street. Some game falls out of her mouth.

Terrence, you can't buy the gas station 'cause a few years ago the city bought they sidewalk for like 1.5 million, and they not gon' sell it back to you. If they did it would cost more than the store is worth and boy what did I tell you about managing your money right? The Arabs who own that store may not be from here but they know what Black people like. All they have to do is call home and tell they families to open up a shop in some Black neighborhood and their money would be endless.

We walk past the market and she says, Now son, you might be able to buy this. The thing is the gas station can't sell tobacco no more so what the market owners do? Opened up a tobacco joint right next door. See. They know what Black people like. They basically a whole monopoly for the next twelve blocks for Black people who don't got no car 'cause why go through the trouble of finding a ride when you can get your swishers and milk right across the street.

And as she says this she's sweating. And I'm sweating. I wanna say it's 'cause we just did laps around Marydale Lake like six times but I know it's really 'cause I must've walked through that boy's ghost. My mom says, We should've crossed the street, I usually cross the street when I walk by myself and I pass that store. They ain't even close the store when he was shot, Mom. Just carried on business as usual. They don't wanna lose money, she says. I get new energy and tell my mom I'ma buy that store one day. Not 'cause I particularly care about business and profit, but cause buying it is the only thing that's right. She says the owner would probably just ask their brother to save them a spot next door and I say I'll buy that too. I don't how I'll get the money, but I will, and I'ma buy that too.

The wind tugs at the remains of a balloon and my mom says, That boy was just standing around up here all day doing nothing. I know, I say, 'cause Ray J knew that boy. He ain't know his name or nothing but he knew him. He said the weed he sold was decent and the boy would just be posted up at the market everyday like clockwork. They ain't even close the store, Mom. They don't even care. I know, Son, she says. That's why I bought this house. So if you ever need help you and your sister won't never have to ask anybody else for nothing when I'm gone.

Cleveland and Chicago: A Tale of Four Cities

MARK V. REYNOLDS

Berlin had a wall. Cleveland has a river.

The Cuyahoga River slinks its way northward from about fifty miles southeast of downtown Cleveland, eventually emptying into Lake Erie (Cleveland was founded where the river and lake converge). On its way to the lake, it flows just west of the main part of downtown, through what used to be an industrial area, the Flats, now home to nightclubs and condos. But for years, the river has been like Berlin's wall to Clevelanders.

The Cuyahoga essentially divides Cleveland into the East Side and the West Side. But the divisions between those two sides aren't just geographical, dictated by nature's path. Once you clear the downtown area, the East Side is where the black folk live, and the West Side is where the white folk live. There are exceptions—some white folk live in ethnic neighborhoods on the southern tip of the East Side and the northeastern edge by the lake; there is a long-standing pocket of black folks on the far West Side—but East is essentially black and West is essentially white. It has been this way since everyone I know can remember.

That hasn't kept black Clevelanders from living full lives. We've seldom needed to go any further west than downtown for anything we needed, unless we worked on the other side of town. We've always had our own shopping, our own nightlife, our own movie theaters, our own churches, our own parks and playgrounds, even our own public transportation (tellingly, none of the east-west bus lines transverse the entire city, they all end downtown and then go back out where they came from). We've had our older neighborhoods where large, sprawling houses still stand, our sturdy working-class neighborhoods, our newer areas where the growing black middle class settled in the '50s and '60s, our stretches of poverty and despair. We've had our world on the East Side, and most of us presumed whites had theirs on the West Side.

During my youth, no one dared cross town because racism was rampant. Whatever specific incidents that fueled those perceptions had become either distant memories and/or urban legends by the time I came along in the '60s. Still, no black person risked getting stuck on the West Side for any reason, especially after dark. That was the message ingrained in me by my parents, who were both born and raised in Cleveland. That was the message I carried even while going to an integrated suburban high school—of course, it was an eastern suburb; even the suburbs adhered to the balkanized racial geography.

That racial geography stemmed in large part from the city's balkanized racial history. There were two different groups of white people to contend with: the old-money gentry, controllers of the business and political arenas and patrons of culture; and European immigrants—Polish, Irish, Italian, Slovakian, German and so on—who assimilated into non-ethnic, all-American whiteness and gained positions of power in the police and fire departments, trade unions, and even the Catholic Church. In their respective ways, neither group made it any easier for the black community, which began to swell in the 1910s as the Great Migration brought impoverished southern blacks northward to Cleveland and other booming Midwestern industrial meccas. Not until the late '60s was there enough of a critical mass for black people to achieve civic power, with the election of Carl Stokes as mayor in 1967. But none of the black political leadership since then has dislodged the city's intractable racial divides.

It was not until I returned home after college that I allowed myself the slightest curiosity about the West Side. By then, I'd learned a lot more about the city's segregated history, and that there were white people on the West Side who were just as keenly aware of it as I was. Feeling more emboldened, I started to (carefully) explore the city past downtown I'd never known. Safer, cultural spots at first—the nightclubs in the Flats, various spots not too far from the West Side Market. It was obvious that economic discrepancies still existed—the stretches of poverty and despair were much less plentiful on the West Side. But as Cleveland's main economy changed in the late '80s and '90s from industrial to professional, with most of the investment happening either in or near downtown or in the area between Cleveland Clinic and University Circle, both sides of town started looking the same to me—which by the '00s was economically depressed. But the ingrained segregation, I suspect, prevented a lot of folks on either side of the river from seeing that for themselves.

Once, I entertained the thought of moving to the West Side, in search of a cheaper apartment in a less dodgy neighborhood. I had a friend who lived in Tremont, a formerly ethnic neighborhood that started experiencing gentrification in the late '80s, and thought there might be a spot there for me, in a part of town I'd never before seen. But my parents, well more than set in their ways by then, flatly announced they would never visit me if I moved away from the East Side, so that was that. Indeed, very few people I know of grew up on one side of town and ended up living on the other—and they're all white.

By the time my family and I moved to Chicago in 2006, Cleveland's essential segregation just was, economic circumstances be damned. I had no idea growing up segregated would make transitioning to this larger metropolis that much easier.

಄

A few years after moving to Chicago, there was the Christmastime story of a young black girl who wanted to do something special for her mom. She had occasion to be downtown, amongst its tall, shiny buildings and places of wealth and affluence, and wondered what it would be like for her mom to get to be inside one of them sometime. So, she wrote a letter to Santa Claus asking for a night in a fancy hotel for her mom. Through the auspices of the Chicago Post Office's "Operation Santa" program, one of those fancy hotels granted that wish.

Something about that heartwarming story struck me as odd. How could anyone not know what those big downtown buildings were like? I'd lived in cities with massive downtowns before—not just Cleveland but also Philadelphia and Atlanta for brief periods—and local features aside, they're all the same. Awe-inspiring on one level, but no big deal once you're used to it. Then I learned how some black folks really weren't used to it, at all. The more I got to know the city, and black Chicagoans, the more I realized how big the chasm here is between engaged and disengaged, rich and poor, black and white.

Across the North Side, where the white folk live, there are numerous post-gentrified neighborhoods, million-dollar condos, fancy restaurants, bespoke retail, numerous food markets, and well-resourced schools. Across the South and West Sides, where the black folk live, there are stretches and stretches where people, property, and commerce used to be, but just emptiness now. Residential and commercial development, if it exists at all, tends to cluster in areas where some level of economic stability already exists, not in the areas that could most immediately use a spark. All is not quite so summarily bleak: there are many spots where long-held neighborhood pride and stability are evident, and many entrepreneurs and organizations are working to establish new community pillars. But the job set out for them is very large, indeed.

This is all the result of Chicago's notorious segregation and racist housing patterns, which confined the rapidly growing black population to a narrow strip of the South Side as the Great Migration took hold, and then repelled them viciously when they dared expand their horizons. This is the city where Dr. Martin Luther King got an eye-opening taste of northern, big city-style racism back in 1966. Things are better now, if you count that Chicago has elected two black mayors since those days, and was the political seat of Illinois' two black elected U.S. Senators (one of whom, you may have heard, went on to be president). And there are black people here who have navigated the heights of the business community, and not just Oprah. But the level of civic economic commitments on the South and West Sides is all but invisible, compared to that in downtown and on the North Side.

So why would black folk know their way around the North Side, or even downtown, if their job didn't take them there? The message that's been ingrained in black souls here for a century and counting is a simple one: "These places where people have money are not for you. Stay where you belong." In this construction, Roosevelt Road serves as the de facto line between North Side (and downtown) and the South Side, just as the Cuyahoga divides black from white in Cleveland.

And once I recognized that, the way Chicago is instantly made sense. It's built largely around the same essential message ingrained in me as a youth in Cleveland. Yes, there is richness and wonder and pride and solidarity in knowing your part of town enjoys a glorious history and ongoing vitality despite its many challenges (both cities can claim black heroes and she-roes in every field of endeavor). But there is also the ever-present danger of self-censoring ambition and mobility, the knowledge that you might be able to conquer the world from your humble 'hood, but might feel culturally adrift and physically unsafe half an hour away from your house, in merely a different part of the city you call home.

And just like in Cleveland, that sense is fostered here by a long-standing, virtually identical power imbalance between black and white, both politically and economically. Chicago too had rich white fathers who ran commerce and politics and bankrolled high culture, and also generations of European immigrants who laid down the law (and, thanks to Chicago-style patronage, handed out the government jobs). If there are any differences, it might be that racism in Chicago was even more virulent than it was in Cleveland, which might explain why Chicago was not able to elect a black mayor until 1983, well after many major American cities.

In that light, it is no accident that Chicago and Cleveland have historically been two of the most segregated cities in America. It is no accident that the result of that segregation in both cases are cities split in two psychically, cities of self-contained, unequal halves where boundaries are felt and lived, respected if not feared, but seen and surmounted not nearly often enough.

Thus did it become easier to learn my way around my new home, not just logistically but also holistically. Racial divides, sadly, translate rather easily from one locale to the next. But that knowledge didn't and doesn't make it any easier to deal with the historic reality of life for black Chicagoans. More than once, as I learned more about the city's racist history and its lingering vestiges, part of me would wonder why folk didn't just march downtown and burn the Loop to the ground. Then I'd remember that many of the very same things happened in Cleveland over the years, and no one destroyed that downtown either.

Berlin had a wall, but they took to it with hammers and pick-axes and tore it down. Cleveland and Chicago have walls too, but not the kind you can tear down with a pickaxe. They've been erected in places that are harder to reach than a river or a street: bitter, entrenched hearts and minds, both black and white, going back for generations, on either side of town.

Disclaimer: The author used to work for the U.S. Postal Service in Chicago, including the "Operation Santa" program, but not on the specific event discussed here.

Peoria, Pryor, and Me

TERRION L. WILLIAMSON

At the intersection of State and Washington Streets in the Warehouse District of downtown Peoria, a city of about 115,000 that sits halfway between Chicago and St. Louis on the Illinois River, stands a nine-foot-tall bronze likeness of the city's most infamous native son. If you were just a casual visitor, perhaps in town to hang out along the up-and-coming riverfront or to visit Caterpillar, the Fortune 500 company that, until it's recent move to the outskirts of Chicago, was headquartered in the city, you would be forgiven for thinking this actually makes sense. *Of course* Peoria would memorialize Richard Pryor, arguably the single most culturally significant Peorian of all time, and inarguably one of the most significant figures in African-American cultural history of the twentieth century. As a visitor, you might not be aware that this homage to Pryor, erected almost ten years after the comedian's death, was years in the making—many more than the nine or so it took local artist Preston Jackson to see the sculpture fully realized—and that "Richard Pryor—More Than Just a Comedian," the sculpture's official name, is ultimately an artifact of Peoria's belated attempt at reconciling the foul-mouthed, woman- and drug-abusing comedian-cum-social critic (or perhaps it's the other way around?) with its image of itself as a model American city where, as the saying goes, it must "play" if it is to play at all.

I was born nearly forty years after Pryor into a Peoria that seemingly wanted to rid itself of any memory of its singular superstar much as it had constructed over any trace of the red-light district where he spent the first decade or so of his life. I consequently had little frame of reference for Pryor the Peorian until after I left home for college when I came to know that for many people, particularly black folks of a certain age, he was the principle, and often only, point of reference for my hometown. Among the things Pryor opined about Peoria was that it was only a model city insofar as it "had the niggers under control." This sort of quip did nothing to endear Pryor to his hometown critics, of course, but when you consider that in the past several years Peoria has been designated an "All-America City"* while also being named one of the worst—even, at one point, *the* worst—cities for black Americans in the country,** the prescient guerilla intellectualism underlying Pryor's act is brought into sharp relief.

I was raised in a decidedly Christian household where I was shielded from much of what Pryor came to know intimately in his own childhood, which, as his biographers never fail to mention, was largely spent in the brothels owned by his grandmother, Marie Carter. Though I, like Pryor, was in my late teens when I left home, when I left it was to attend first college then law school and eventually graduate school, while Pryor's sojourns along the way to superstar status included a stint in the US Army, a tour of the Chitlin Circuit, and a residency in Greenwich Village. But while Richard Pryor might seem a peculiar point of departure for me, a churchgirl-turned-college professor, it is in his brazen commentary and his obscene, autobiographical, profanity-laden stage routines that I have found something of a life I know—something that the conventions of academia can sometimes gesture toward but that, for me, have only been fully embodied in the place and the people I know of as home.

I came up "down the hill" on Peoria's predominately black South Side which, like most such places, is the most economically depleted, resource-deprived neighborhood in the entire city. I attended Harrison Primary School, Trewyn Middle School, and Manual High School, all of which have since been restructured due to their failure to meet the mandates of standardized testing and other governmental assessments. Then and now (my parents still live in my childhood home) the South Side is largely seen as Peoria's site of consummate failure, the place from which one must flee in order to be understood as successful or "upwardly mobile." Then and now the South Side is talked about as a neighborhood almost wholly given over to criminality and vice, where one's life might be snuffed out at any given moment. Then, and most certainly now, certain political figures and their stand-ins imagine that what it must be like to live in communities like the South Side of Peoria where I once lived, the West Side of Chicago where I worked my way through college, or North Minneapolis where I currently make my home, are reducible to "hell," as if our lives are conditioned by nothing other than absolute terror, as if all we need is an all-knowing

---

*According to the website of the National Civic League, which grants the All-America City award, an All-America City is one that uses "inclusive civil engagement to address critical issues and create stronger connections among residents, businesses and nonprofit and government leaders." Peoria has won the award four times, the last time in 2013.

** Peoria has been named on the annual list of the "Worst Cities for Black Americans" developed by the financial news site 24/7 Wall St. since its inception in 2015. Peoria has been ranked as high as number one, in 2016, and as low as number seven, in 2019.

(usually white, probably male) savior to come rescue us from ourselves.

Although it is true that I left Peoria as a young person and have yet to return but for holidays and the occasional visit, literary scholar Hortense Spillers reminds us in her essay "*The Crisis of the Negro Intellectual: A Post-Date*" that just because we do not live *in* a place doesn't mean that we are not *of* a place. Here, then, is Richard Pryor's truest legacy. While he might have mocked and critiqued Peoria, and left never to permanently return again, he never held himself apart from it. Indeed, what others took as the detritus of black life he took as its very substance, and in his 1994 autobiography *Pryor Convictions* he argued that people like the hustlers, prostitutes, winos, and pimps who he grew up with and around, and who he continued to surround himself with throughout his life, were people who "knew stuff worth knowing."

Perhaps for those who know nothing of what it means to live on the "black side" of town (or who have convinced themselves that they have "risen above" such circumstance), it is difficult if not impossible to imagine that people like Peoria's black South Siders—who aren't just thugs and gangsters but are also (like my mom) bookkeepers and (like my best friend) nurses and (like my stepdad) business owners and everything else in between (including, yes, thugs and gangsters)—know something worth knowing. And what they know is that while their lives ain't no parts of easy, they are fundamentally irreducible to their worst days or their hardest moments. What they know is that black social life is life that is lived *in spite of.*

If you believe the rhetoric about the "inner city" which would suggest that financial insecurity and boarded-up homes and broken-down schools and food deserts and "the criminal element" and chronic joblessness means that we don't have joy here, or that we don't have (self-) love here, or that we don't have fellowship here, or that we don't have scholarship here, or that we don't have safety here, then, as the wino said to the junkie in a certain Richard Pryor skit, "that shit done made you null and void." While "hood life" certainly does not always acquiesce to the demands of the state or the protocols of the "proper" (although very often it does just that), it is this very capacity for fugitivity, or what we might otherwise call making a way out of no way, that is, at least according to the life I have lived, the very enabling condition of home. And I wouldn't have it any other way.

An earlier version of this essay was published in Belt Magazine *on October 13, 2016.*

Detroit: Love of My Life

COURTNEY WISE RANDOLPH

Just like my mama, Detroit loves me for real. She's held me up when I least deserved it, even when I wished to have been born and raised elsewhere.

I was around thirteen when I stopped appreciating the city for itself and what it offered me. I'd silently witnessed conversations among people I thought were important that left me believing I'd never be a success unless I escaped Detroit. I had to graduate from high school (preferably Cass Tech) with a full-ride to college, use that time to travel the world and join some reputable social circles, then employ said connections to secure a job that would get me as far away from Detroit as possible. I'd stack a lot of money until approximately age thirty-eight when I'd be nearly rich enough to retire. At that point I could afford to pause my ascent to power long enough to co-parent a child—identical twins?—with a six-foot or taller, dark-skinned, muscle-bound man with close-cropped kinky curls or shoulder-length locs, athletic skill, and healthy stock options. Tall and dark because of course; stock options because I read it in a magazine somewhere. I didn't have a good vision about what made a good partner or parent. I wasn't even appropriately concerned about a kind heart, generous spirit, or frankly the other person's desire to raise a life in this world.

I'd have to accomplish those things at a premier school like Howard or Spelman and only return to Detroit annually for Mother's Day, my Mama's birthday, and alternating Thanksgivings and Christmases. So I graduated from Cass Tech and attended my dream university—Howard—on a full tuition and partial room scholarship. But as you might expect from an essay like this one, my naïve plan unwound from there. I'd spent my childhood and adolescence tethered to a miserable and formidable father, and I'd wrapped up high school by binding myself to a young man just like him. I bumbled about in D.C. for four years, was virtually lifted from a mental abyss by a trio of angels just before I attempted to end my life, got a couple of lifelong friends out of the experience, and left in the spring of 2006 with no degree. I returned to Detroit feeling embarrassed and defeated and vowed to myself I'd be enrolled in arts school in Chicago by that fall to pursue my truest passions. Not because Chicago was the Promised Land but because Detroit was certainly a graveyard.

By then though, my Mama had spent thousands of dollars financing my depressive self-destruction and she neither desired nor could afford for me to ease further down said road on her dime. I had to figure something else out. City Year is where I turned. I wasn't too serious about a service year, but I needed to buy myself time to figure out how I'd get out of Detroit and the scholarship option at the end of the year sounded like a good deal. I interviewed well enough to be offered a spot in Detroit's seventh City Year Corps. At the end of my first full day of service, my whole life changed.

At the time, City Year wasn't solely focused on improving educational outcomes for Detroit's public-school students. It was also committed to providing bold leadership opportunities for its extremely young corps (comprised of adolescents and young adults aged 17 to 24), and it required twice-monthly collaborative community service events. Five years earlier, I'd shaken my head at the idealistic teens from Detroit Summer who'd come knocking on my front door. I had no clue about Jimmy and Grace Boggs, the legendary activists who founded Detroit Summer in 1992 and already inspired generations of youth to create the Detroit in which they wanted to live through creative and sustainable solutions. I just thought they were braver than they should've been (re: a teensy bit stupid) to walk up and down my block telling people to come to a gathering in the park. Wasn't it dangerous for them to do so? Now City Year was telling me I had to go find people like those teens to work with in Detroit's neighborhoods because our power combined with theirs made Detroit great. I had to believe in the power of Detroit's citizens—including me—to rewrite the city's public narrative and then go do it. It was a tough sell, but I bought it. And as true to life as ever, I haven't been the same since.

I remembered uncomfortably chuckling at a security officer's suggestion that I might shoot at people who annoyed me while I once ate at Pentagon City mall. It seems all he knew was Detroit's reputation for murder. But getting to work in Detroit's communities made me start talking back. I told people about how the Artist's Village, Motor City Blight Busters, Motor City Java, and Sweet Potato Sensations were prime examples of tremendous light in Brightmoor, a far westside neighborhood once described as "Blightmoor"—in *The Detroit News* of all places. I took mediation classes and met artist-entrepreneurs like the Smile Brand's Philip Simpson when one of his first ventures—Freshman Clothing—breathed life into Downtown. I had the nerve to get hype about the Heidelberg Project, and later I went on to teach elementary school (not for long though—that ain't for me).

I worked briefly in the neighborhood office of then Michigan State Representative Rashida Tlaib. I got to hear Maureen Taylor and Marian Kramer speak. I even met Grace Lee Boggs—just a few years after I shook my head at those idealistic kids she inspired through Detroit Summer. Each of those interactions taught my heart, enriched my life, and fed my body—for real. I got jobs that paid my bills and bought my groceries throughout all of that. I hear people still speak ill on Detroit and only hear Grace saying, "I feel so sorry for people who are not living in Detroit."

I tell myself I'm so glad my life flipped upside down and brought me back home. I feel so sorry for people who think they can't build a life of impact outside of New York or L.A. And with all due respect to one of my favorite places on earth, NYC, its folks really need to bring it down a notch. Once, while on a six-week extended stay in New York, a woman asked me how I expected to find my way back home on the train alone since I was from Detroit. I could barely believe she fixed her mouth to say that. It was like she thought of my city as a deserted land and those of us who momentarily stepped out had to relearn how to navigate civilization. But let's be real—Detroit didn't stop producing hitmakers when Motown moved its headquarters to LA. Besides, I'd navigated the DDOT—Detroit's notorious Department of Transportation in the late '90s and early '00s—in comparison, the MTA was a luxury. Her question hit me in the gut though and made me realize such sentiments are as foolish as I used to be about what's always been here.

In the spring of 2006, right after I promised myself I'd re-secure the life I'd let slip away by escaping Detroit again, I met a man. I told him I liked him, but I wasn't interested in tying myself down to another person or this place. He needed to keep it cool and focus on fun (re: sex in the summertime). Just like Detroit, with a twinkle in his eye, he smiled and nodded okay, knowing the whole while that I'd gladly share as much life with him as God would allow.

Besides, how could I leave so soon after Detroit freely gave me so many new opportunities to grow up? Asking only to witness some of my joy in experiencing in return?

So this still is where I remain. At home. In Detroit. In a love as rooted as ever in the city that's loved me all my days. Where I would be without Detroit is something I have at times wondered, but am glad I'll never know.

On Spades, Queerness, and the Things We Learn from Our Grandmothers*

KIDIOCUS KING-CARROLL

I grew up in the 5000-block of Milwaukee's North Side, a black city within the city. Milwaukee is frequently cited as one of the worst places in the country to be black by outlets like *24/7 Wall Street* and *NPR.com*. These publications often point to racialized hypersegregation, mass incarceration, and poor educational outcomes as indicators of the untenable living situation for black Milwaukeeans. Still, these indices are not the first thing that comes to mind when I think of my home. When I think of home in the Midwest and Milwaukee, I often think of my Grandma, Susan (pronounced sue-ZAN). This is a dichotomous line of reasoning within itself because she hates the Midwest. Since my birth, she has consistently moved between Milwaukee and her birthplace in the Arkansas Delta. Yet, much of my understanding of Milwaukee (and the Midwest) as my home stems from the intellectual, cultural, and practical knowledge that my grandma imparted to me over games of Spades in my parent's house on the city's North Side.

Grandma Susan is an earnest Spades player, and she has no tolerance for cheating or lazy playing. My brother and I were often chastised for reneging (a form of cheating) or being too easy to beat—she seemed to find a particular joy in calling us out. She taught us to play, and it always felt like more than a game—it was an experience of familial bonding that I never had the grammar to articulate until I was well into adulthood. We would play for hours, and I eventually became a proficient Spades player with time, but I've never managed to be as good as my grandma. She has a natural talent for besting her opponents that I've never managed to recreate. For my grandma, the game was a means of imparting knowledge about our family and the world around us.

---

*I would like to thank Hana Maruyama, Caitlin Gunn, and Dr. Terrion Williamson for their help in writing this piece. Additionally, I would like to thank my grandmother, Ruley "Susan" King, for teaching me everything that I know about Spades.

My grandma also has a strong affinity for the macabre—we'd spend hours playing Spades and watching Bette Davis psychological thrillers like *Whatever Happened to Baby Jane* and *Hush…Hush, Sweet Charlotte*, or she'd tell us real-life horror stories about men like the infamous Milwaukee serial killer, Jeffrey Dahmer. "Yeah, boy," she'd say. "I lived right down the street from him—he worked at a candy factory and used to cut up those men that he killed and sell their meat to local restaurants. Folks were eating human flesh." I've never been able to ascertain as to whether these stories were a distraction tactic or if my memories of those card games, films, and her stories have coalesced into distinct units that actually occurred at discrete moments throughout my childhood. What I do know is that my grandma is known for her prowess at the cards table, her love of horror, and her imaginative, sometimes hyperbolic storytelling. I'd suggest that my grandma's card playing and the social and cultural knowledge that she'd impart over those games were part of a black feminist practice. I have never heard her use the word "feminist" to describe how she lives within herself and interacts with the world. Still, there doesn't have to be an intention for an act to be a black feminist act or practice. What I do know is that the things that I learned from her through those Spades games were a way for her to teach me about the world and the meaning of home.

The act of playing Spades is about fun, but it is also about communality and organic knowledge building—I learned many things about pop culture and black social life over those card games that I'd argue aided in the development of my own queer cultural sensibility. To paraphrase the scholar E. Patrick Johnson, everything I learned about being queer, I learned from my grandma (or almost). This is not a statement that she might agree with, but I would say that the sociality that occurred over those card games was queer. Learning camp culture and enjoying horror over a set of cards with your grandmother is queer. Since my childhood, I've come to understand that those experiences with my Grandma Susan were not necessarily atypical. By which I mean that I've met many black folks who have acknowledged that some of their understanding of the world emanates from what they learned at a Spades table. When I think of Spades and my childhood in Milwaukee, I remember the abundance of fried fish, spaghetti, and brown liquor that took the form of Crown Royal, Canadian Club, or Hennessy. And you might also have a can of Milwaukee's Best, Miller, or Old Milwaukee, and you would play as if your life depended on it. And if you don't know how to play Spades, then you don't know how to play Spades. I am not suggesting that Spades is particular to the Midwest or black people, but I do know that it originated in Cincinnati and that it is serious business amongst black folks.

A game of Spades is about joy and existing in community with family and friends. Life happens over a game of Spades: people drink and play the dozens, they laugh, and they fight, they gossip, and they plan for the future. I've met black folks from the Midwest and elsewhere who've told me that they learned to count and became attuned to reading facial language over games of Spades, often in scenarios similar to the games that I witnessed as a child growing up in Milwaukee. I came into being in the Midwest and my understanding of it as home and who I am as a black gay man stems, in part, from something as seemingly innocuous and mundane as a game of Spades. Home can be a place of mundanity and a site of knowledge that informs how we live long after we've left.

Tracing Water, Memory, and Change

NJAIMEH NJIE

The author overlooking the Ohio River on the North Side section of the Three Rivers Heritage Trail off of Route 65 in Pittsburgh.

I live right above the Ohio River, off of a thoroughfare called the Ohio River Boulevard. It is one section of Route 65–a fifty-one-mile stretch of highway that travels from downtown Pittsburgh, northwest to the city of New Castle. The route spans three counties, three major rivers and several neighborhoods, boroughs, towns and tributaries as it makes its way through Western Pennsylvania's industrial belt.

For me, living so close to the Ohio River evokes mixed feelings. The river trail that I like to walk along near my apartment is scenic, yet long stretches of it are flanked by the railroad, warehouses and industrial sites on either side. At home, I drink water from a filtered pitcher because of years of elevated lead levels in Pittsburgh's water, and I regularly learn about new water threats in the region. I feel a constant push and pull between the things that are good for me and the things that can harm me, but I know my perspective is just one of many.

View of Route 65 from Ambridge, Pennsylvania.

My work focuses on how history shapes the contemporary experiences of Black people in the industrial Midwest, and I've been thinking about water as a gateway to explore the deeper forces that shape the lives and livelihoods of Black people in this region.

Black residents have traditionally lived close to the waterways — sometimes by choice, but often because of racist housing and land-use policies.

Over the years, the proximity to water allowed access to transit, jobs, bathing, washing, fishing and leisure, but it also placed these communities at a disproportionate risk for flooding, pollution, disease and other issues caused by water.

This history is encapsulated in the area that Route 65 spans. Like the rivers, it is a sort of connective tissue, linking people and places across the region.

I set out to talk to Black residents living in communities along and near Route 65 about where they live and their experiences in these places, in the context of their connections to water.

What you'll read and see isn't a definitive account of Black life in this area. Instead, it will present the stories of a few people, in a few places, and uses water as an entry point to the complex social, political and economic context of the region.

Olivia Bennett on Mt. Pleasant Road in Pittsburgh's Northview Heights neighborhood. Bennett won the Nov. 5, 2019 election for the District 13 seat on the Allegheny County Council.

Bennett: I started doing research and learning more about what County Council does—what they actually have purview over. I started unfolding all of this stuff like environmental justice, Port Authority, Health Department, the jail, and it's like, oh—there's a whole lot of work that can be done in this position that hasn't been getting done, that actually impacts people that look like me.

"I describe [environmental justice] as being very mindful of what our actions each day, in our livelihoods, how that impacts our environment… But, I also look at it as how it impacts different communities in different ways. A lot of these pollut[ing] plants…they typically go into areas that are predominantly poor and predominantly communities of color. They try to build pipelines on sacred land. If you want the benefits from these plants to benefit the whole, then why are we not putting these plants in other places? Why are they specifically targeted to go to places that can't typically advocate for themselves?

"One of the things I've been fighting [in Northview Heights] is slow repairs. I mean, my courtyard always floods every time it rains. They're supposed to be redoing it. They were supposed to be doing it for the last five years. So that type of thing, those types of fights. Just because we are living in public housing does not make us any less human. …How can we make sure that everybody's coming along at the same rate to be able to fight against this? What creativity can we come along with to allow people to take ownership and be given the tools?"

Jamie Younger working inside Young Brothers Bar, on the border of the Woods Run and Brighton Heights neighborhoods of Pittsburgh. Young Brothers sits about a mile from the county's ALCOSAN water treatment facility.

Younger: "Historically, Black people didn't cross over Woods Run Avenue in my father's time. At the time I went to [high school], when we came out of school at the end of the day, it seemed like the Black people walked right, and the white people walked left down this way. I never made that left, even to explore or venture. I bought a house up here after getting outta college and been here ever since.

"When I first moved up here, when the wind blew, the smell was vicious. It would stop you in your tracks, and you'd be like, 'Oh that ALCOSAN stinks.' I don't know what they've done over the years to mitigate that because it's not as bad … except maybe after a lot of rain and then the wind blows. But I haven't said that in a while.

"…It definitely keeps evolving geographically where Black folks are at. Black folks are finding it hard to live in the city. They're finding it hard to find affordable housing within the city, and they're going out to places like McKees Rocks … out into Beaver County, Ambridge. So it's like, I don't know—unless you own a home, I don't know where you're gonna go soon in the city, especially within the North Side of the city. It's definitely becoming a challenge to find affordable, quality spaces to live within the city boundaries. It's forever changing."

Terry Stenhouse (left) works with Lethera Harrison behind the counter of Annie Lee's Southern Kitchen.

Stenhouse: "I've always been kinda leery about the quality of the drinking water. I went to school, I took my apprenticeship. I've been doing plumbing off and on since I was like nineteen. You know, working on the pipes and seeing cross sections of different pipes, and even when I was in the military and I purified water, I've always been kinda skeptical about the testing and the quality of the water. I really don't have too much faith in the purification process, but once the water is purified and they run it through the piping system, in my eyes, it's re-contaminated.

"You know, we all need water. It's essential for life, so everyone's connected to it ... but at the same time, lately [for] something that's supposed to be essential to life, [it] has been causing a lot of health problems. I mean we deal with water every day here at the restaurant. We cook with water, we have a filter on it. I just think we need to get better with the water all around. I don't really think that it's anyone's fault to blame, because when these systems were put in, the information we have now wasn't available. I don't think it was done on purpose ... it's just being swept under the rug in terms of correcting the problem. So that's what I think."

Douglas: "I was born in Rochester, Pa., not too far from where we're sitting right now. I was born in 1930. Rochester, in the nineteenth century, was one of the most important towns around because it's at the point where the Ohio River turns to go southwest. It gets to Rochester and the Beaver River runs into the Ohio at that point. And that's why today Rochester has five major highways that go through it because of that juncture. It was also because the trains.

Elizabeth "Betty" Asche Douglas is an art-culture historian, retired professor, artist and jazz performer. Here she is pictured in her studio in Rochester, Pennsylvania.

"My father was an electronic technician. He started out as a radio man, repairing and making radios and so forth. How we got to Beaver Falls, I don't know, but my first memories of life were in the first house we lived in in Beaver Falls, because it was on First Avenue. Across the street from First Avenue were the railroad tracks, and across from the railroad tracks was the river. So one of my earliest memories is of my father taking me by the hand and walking me down First Avenue, towards the train station there, and it was during the spring of the year of the great floods in Western Pennsylvania—'37, I think. He said, 'When the water gets up to there [she indicated the high-water level with her hand] we will have to leave.' So my first childhood memory is watching the river in the springtime to see how high the water was getting because the houses on First Avenue would be the first ones to go over.

"The river was very important to Black boys especially because there were no swimming pools in Beaver Valley that would allow Black boys to swim in them. So every year there would be a Black kid that drowned in the river because they went down to the river to swim. I don't think the people thought about pollution in those days. And I don't know how garbage or waste or sewage was treated. When you're a kid, you don't think about that. The only thing you knew is you flushed the toilet and it goes away. Where it goes, you don't think about."

Zeigler: "[I'm] originally from New York, but I grew up about a mile down the road from the pool, a place called Koppel. Small town. [Growing up in] Koppel, Beaver Falls, New Brighton—there was always something to do. You could always find a pickup game when it came to basketball or baseball, Wiffle ball … I used to pass here all the time, drive past, ride my back past, because I used to ride my bike all the way from Koppel to New Brighton, just to go play basketball. So I used to ride by and see tons of people outside. The city had owned the property. Trying to maintain the city and the property became too much for them, so they turned the pool over to the YMCA. That just became too much, so they just decided to shut it down.

"I just turned my life around six years ago. So before all that it's been my dream to re-open all of this, but I didn't know how—and I knew people wasn't gonna take a drug dealer serious. As I kept growing and maturing, I saw that people started respecting me a lot more. I seen that I was getting my reputation back. So I was riding by one day and … I just took a glance at it and a light bulb went off, and I said, 'I believe that I can pull this off.' And three years later, [we're] super close.

"My vision is to get these kids off the street. My vision is to give them some type of structure. What about the kids that don't play football, that don't play baseball, that don't play basketball? What about the kids that the parents don't have the funds at all? So all they got is these drug dealers that's their influences and the streets that's their influences. Nobody's really thinking about that. That was my biggest problem, being a follower. Now I'm a leader, and I'm trying to give them a blueprint so they don't have to take that same path that I took. This is a start right here. I'm here. I'm not going anywhere either."

Hogans: "My father worked in the steel mills. So did my grandfather and so did my uncle. …[The Shenango] is the river that goes down through

Tyrone Zeigler outside of the Beaver Falls wave pool. Zeigler is project manager of the Tigerland Wave Pool initiative, through the Beaver County Community Development Corporation. Zeigler is spearheading fundraising efforts to repair and re-open the pool.

the middle of New Castle. So, because of the way that the [mills] would use the water, the river was extremely polluted. It was something you ignored. We just know that oftentimes we did not use the water. We never drank from the water. There was a place that we could swim. It was called El Rio Beach, which is funny, 'cause it's … still considered to be in the middle of New Castle.

"People—Black people especially—would go in the summertime, and we would run across and splash across. If the water was high enough, we'd ride the rapids down across the rocks in the creek. When the rain would come, the sewers would wash out and we'd play in the open sewers they were developing 'cause the water was clean, and it was flowing. Very dangerous. We didn't realize it, but that's what we did to keep cool in the summer.

"When I was seventeen, eighteen years old, I left here because the economic plight was so bad. It was so hard to get a job. You know the steel mills, they fluctuated like the tide. Some days you could not *not* get a job. And then there were other times where they would do layoffs and shutdowns and cut back on production. By the time 1975 came around, when I was getting ready to graduate, there was nothing for me to do as a Black person that I knew of except for work in the grocery store or flip burgers.

"[Now] I'm assigned here, by our Bishop and my vision of God. I wanna do things that make health happen. I want to create a garden—two of them. There are natural springs in New Castle. I want to create a water treatment plant where we create our own bottled water. My hope for the role of the church is that we awaken people to the need for economic and spiritual and social empowerment. New Castle has declined. It's shrunk in population base. The population is much older. That's the challenge for the church: how to be a relevant agent of change for the better, where harmony and a healthy existence can occur. And my vision and hope is to create that."

Rev. William Hogans is pictured addressing the congregation at St. Luke during the kickoff gospel event for the church's 175th anniversary weekend celebration in September 2019.

Octavia Payne: "I'm from North Carolina and I met my husband at Knoxville College. We were married and we came here to New Castle in 1970. New Castle was my husband's home. I had my baby with me, and that was Ursula. And we came here, we taught school here for 35 years. We had an uncle, Big Jim, who, when we first moved here, we stayed with him. And I remember how rusty the water was because he had well water. We drank it; it was good water! He had big picnics out there, a garden—he had a green thumb. He had a lot of property out there, he liked to cook, and his water was good."

Paulette Booker: "Back then, all our family outings was at his house. I came from Pensacola, Fla. I came up here in January of 1963. This is my father's home, and I've been here ever since. When we were in Florida, we were always surrounded by family and having family get-togethers and family fun, and then when we came here, it was the same thing, so the transition wasn't as bad. And we grew up fishing, too."

Ursula Payne: "My stories about water are kind of folkloric tales. I don't want to say folklore because [my stories] are true, but I always remember the story of my grandfather's brother … who drowned in the Shenango River. I remember family telling stories about that. It was always, 'That's why you don't go by the river or go swimming in the Shenango River because you can get caught up in the currents.' So I remember some of those tragic stories. And the other thing about water I remember is my father, he used to fish all the time. My father and my Uncle Lenny."

James Burley, Jr.: "[I was] born and raised in New Castle, my whole life. I started going fishing, and that's the main thing I do with water. I'd walk the whole Neshannock Creek. …We were pulling in all kinds of fish at the

Pictured left to right: Paulette Booker, Octavia Payne, Ursula Payne, Carl Booker and James Burley, Jr., in Ursula Payne's New Castle home. Octavia Payne is a retired educator and co-founder of the Diamond Girls youth program in New Castle. Her daughter Ursula is the chairperson of the Department of Dance and director of the Frederick Douglass Institute at Slippery Rock University. Paulette and Carl Booker are close relatives of the Paynes, and James Burley, Jr. is a friend and former classmate of Ursula Payne.

time and then all of a sudden they made some regulations and they blocked it off, so we weren't allowed to go for a while. So then we started going to the Shenango River and started doing really good in the Shenango River, then all of a sudden they started blocking, fencing that off, so we couldn't go. There were warnings: Don't eat the fish because of all the mercury. We did it for the fun anyway; we didn't really care about eating them.

Carl Booker: "The water wasn't safe. Most of [the pollution] came from [the factories] up in the Sharon area, but they never update nothing. They put [the warnings] out what, four years ago? They haven't updated it. They say it's still not good, though. I was born and raised here. I don't do nothing 'round the water 'round here [now], but when I was younger we used to swim in it. I lived on the tracks. The West Side, that's what we called it … where the bypass is now."

Octavia Payne: "There was a whole development down there. Not one house down there now. It's highway. They wiped out a whole community down there—but the river's still there."

II.
PAST

History, despite its wrenching pain, cannot be unlived, and if faced with courage, need not be lived again.
—Maya Angelou

(Born in St. Louis, Missouri, 1928)

Slavery, Freedom, and African American Voices in the Midwest

MELISSA STUCKEY

While reading Jon Lauck's essay, "Regionalist Stirrings in the Midwest," in the first issue of *The New Territory*, I was struck by the author's argument that the past century's literary critics largely ignored Midwestern writers. What, I wondered, about the timeless and award-winning work of Toni Morrison? Morrison, like other African American literary luminaries (Langston Hughes, Ralph Ellison and Gwendolyn Brooks, to name just a few) was born in the Midwest, and like them she has devoted a significant portion of her career to examining African American lives in the cities, small towns, hills, valleys and rivers of the region. We miss out on much that is important about the Midwest when we fail to consider the complex narratives of African Americans here.

Morrison's first novel *The Bluest Eye* is set in her birthplace, Lorain, Ohio. She returned to Ohio in *Sula* (1973) and *Beloved* (1987) while also contemplating African American life, history, and memory in Michigan in *Song of Solomon* (1977) and Oklahoma in *Paradise* (1997). Reading *Beloved* is necessary not only for its own sake, but especially when considering the nineteenth-century history of the Midwest.

Set on the banks of the Ohio River just outside Cincinnati, *Beloved's* inspiration was the tragic history of Margaret Garner. In 1856, Garner and her family escaped from slavery in Kentucky by crossing over the frozen Ohio River. They were discovered and, while cornered, Margaret Garner determined to kill her children and herself rather than allow any of them to be reenslaved. She succeeded in killing one child before being captured and imprisoned. Her trial determined neither guilt nor innocence in the death of her daughter, but rather that her Kentucky owner had the right to pursue and recoup his property (the Garner family) even after they had escaped slave territory (Kentucky) and had found refuge in free territory (Ohio). As a result, she and her surviving family members were sold further south.

Morrison uses *Beloved* to create voices for enslaved women like Margaret Garner who were rendered voiceless by laws that denied them the right to read and write, to testify in court, to benefit from their own labor, to legally wed, to control access to their own bodies and to claim their children as their own.

Through the novel, Morrison also helps her audience better appreciate that the histories of slavery and freedom in the United States are neither confined to the American South nor constricted by simplistic Northern-Southern geographical and cultural divisions. Instead, Morrison brings to life the reality that some of the most pressing issues surrounding slavery and freedom in the United States played out in the Middle West.

Slavery and Freedom in the Lower Midwest

For much of the early to mid-1800s, the Lower Midwest was a battleground upon which the future of slavery across the nation was fought. The conflict over slavery was hastened by the 1803 Louisiana Purchase, through which the United States acquired territory that eventually became Missouri, Arkansas, Oklahoma, Kansas, and Nebraska. The first clash, taking place between 1818 and 1820, was over Missouri's admission to statehood as a slave state. It resulted in the Missouri Compromise. The Comprise allowed slavery in Missouri but drew a corner around the area that would one day become Kansas and Nebraska. That corner would be closed to slavery. Like Missouri, however, Arkansas and Indian Territory (later Oklahoma) would also be open to slavery. As a result, between 1810 and 1860, the slave populations in Missouri and Arkansas ballooned from 3,011 to 114,931 and 188 to 111,115, respectively. Oklahoma did not become a state until the twentieth century, but in 1860 more than 8,000 blacks were held in slavery in Indian Territory.

Thirty years later, America's crisis over slavery was again exposed in the Lower Midwest. First, free blacks, including those like Margaret Garner who had escaped slavery and settled in free territory, were put in danger through the passage of the Fugitive Slave Act in 1850. The law allowed anyone to be deputized to aid in capturing any black accused of being a slave. It denied the accused the right to testify in their own defense and provided monetary incentives for courts to determine that blacks were slaves rather than free.

Then in 1854, Congress nullified the Missouri Compromise by passing the Kansas-Nebraska Act. The legislation allowed for citizens of each future state to determine their slave status through the principle of "popular sovereignty," meaning through the electoral process. As a result of the law, pro- and anti-slavery partisans flooded into Kansas and engaged in bloody warfare in order to gain control of the territory in advance of statehood. After years of violence and political battles, Kansas entered the Union as a free state in 1861. Nebraska became a state in 1867, two years after the Civil War settled the question of slavery in the United States.

While important, statistics, legislation, and political battles over slavery only tell a portion of the story. As Toni Morrison reminds us, the human element of slavery can never be overlooked.

Dred Scott and the Pursuit of Freedom

Among the hundreds of thousands of individual stories about slavery, Garner's is just one—lucky to be preserved by Morrison's talented pen and ultimately ending in tragedy. Dred Scott's story, while tragic, endures of its own accord. His lawsuit, filed in circuit court in St. Louis, Missouri, in 1846 and decided by the U.S. Supreme Court in 1856, the same year that Garner attempted her own bid for freedom, made him one of the most important figures in nineteenth-century American history.

Born in Virginia around 1799, Dred Scott was owned by Peter and Elizabeth Blow. Seeking better fortunes, the Blows moved, with their slaves, first to Alabama and then in or around 1830 to St. Louis, Missouri. In 1831, the Blows sold Scott to Army surgeon John Emerson. Between 1831 and 1842, Dred Scott served Emerson in Missouri, Illinois, and at Fort Snelling in the Wisconsin Territory (now Minnesota). The practice of slavery was illegal in the latter two places. During this 12-year period Scott married Harriet Robinson, an enslaved woman. The couple raised two daughters while serving Dr. Emerson and his wife Eliza Irene Sanford, primarily in free territory. The Scotts returned to St. Louis with the Emersons in 1842, and the surgeon died a year later. For several years, Mrs. Emerson hired out the Scotts in St. Louis.

In 1846, however, the Scotts filed suit against Emerson for their freedom and the freedom of their daughters on the grounds that for more than a decade they had lived in territory where slavery was illegal. The Scott family had reason to hope for a successful outcome to their lawsuit. Missouri courts had long been known to follow the doctrine of "once free, always free" in deciding similar cases. Indeed, the Scotts won their initial petition. But an appeals court reversed the decision. More appeals and many delays followed. In the meantime, Emerson remarried and transferred ownership of the Scotts to her brother John Sanford. Finally, a full decade after the original suit was filed, *Dred Scott v. Sandford* (a misspelling of Sanford originating at the time the lawsuit was filed) was argued before the United States Supreme Court.

The Supreme Court heard arguments on the case in 1856 and, on March 6, 1857, it ruled that the Scotts were to remain slaves. In its decision, however, the Court went beyond simply determining the legal status of the Scott family. Instead, it used the ruling to issue a sweeping statement on race and slavery in America. Writing for the Court's majority, Chief Justice Roger B. Taney penned a blistering opinion meant to permanently declass African Americans by denying them U.S. citizenship rights. He also declared that Congress did not have the right to determine the slaveholding status of any portion of the United States. This final opinion further stoked the flames of sectional division over slavery in the Lower Midwest and the across the nation. This fire would not be extinguished until the conclusion of the American Civil War in 1865.

Black Freedom in the Lower Midwest

Although the Scotts lost their legal case, allies purchased and then freed them soon afterward. Having enjoyed scarcely a year of freedom, Dred Scott died of tuberculosis on September 17, 1858. Originally buried in Wesleyan Cemetery in St. Louis, he is now interred in St. Louis's historic Calvary Cemetery.

Harriet Scott, who lived another eighteen years, remained in St. Louis after her husband's death. Pre-war St. Louis was a close-knit community of free blacks and urban slaves. In 1860, half of Missouri's free black population, some 1,800 people, lived in the city. Together they and the 4,340 blacks enslaved there worked hard to create lives for themselves. The urban setting allowed for the creation of valuable community networks. Among these networks were churches like the First African Baptist Church, which operated a secret school even after the Missouri legislature banned education for slaves. For free blacks, St. Louis also provided a measure of safety in the form of safe houses where blacks could hide from slave catchers and kidnappers emboldened by the Fugitive Slave Act.

Harriet Scott lived to see slavery's end. She died on June 17, 1876 and is buried in Greenwood Cemetery in St. Louis. In 2010, a memorial pavilion was constructed on the cemetery's grounds in her honor. In the years immediately following Harriet Scott's death, St. Louis again became a refuge, this time for African Americans seeking to escape anti-black violence and economic and political oppression in Arkansas or the Deep South. The city also became a gateway for blacks heading to Kansas, Nebraska, or other parts of Missouri to homestead, reside in all-black communities, or to live in other urban areas. A separate stream of black people moved directly from the South into Indian Territory in search of the same freedoms and opportunities.

Although African Americans have been minorities for the entirety of their history in the Lower Midwest, their presence and experiences in this space brought forth some of the most critical debates, conversations, and issues that gripped the nation in the nineteenth century. It was the place where questions about slavery and freedom pushed the United States to the brink of war. It was also the place blacks traveled to in search of freedom before and after that war. In short, although the histories of African Americans in the Midwest are widely divergent, taken together they tell a quintessentially American story about the unceasing struggle for freedom.

In Morrison's *Beloved*, Baby Suggs, former slave, matriarch and preacher, says to her congregation, "In this here place, we flesh; flesh that weeps, laughs; flesh that dances on bare feet in grass. Love it. Love it hard." Baby Suggs's message is important for contemporary Midwesterners, writers, historians, and critics, as well. It is incumbent upon all of us to acknowledge, embrace, and—dare I say—love all of the people that make up the Midwest. In this way we fulfill the freedom dreams of Margaret Garner, Dred and Harriet Scott, and all of our Midwestern forebears.

This piece was originally published in The New Territory, *Issue 2.*

Ella Mae: The Personal and the Political

JEFFREY C. WRAY

Ella Mae.

Ella Mae McEwen and Joe Wray were married in Medina, Ohio in 1957. He came north from Chapel Hill, Tennessee to join his brother and work in the town factory. She moved with her family from Lexington, Kentucky into the small black community of Medina located near that factory and the railroad tracks. By 1968 they had built a working-class life and a social life. They had three young boys and looked forward to their future. On a late May night in 1968 that future changed.

A month after the assassination of Martin Luther King, my father Joe Wray was murdered in my small hometown of Medina, Ohio, just south of Cleveland.

I was eight at the time. My two brothers, Joe and Jonathan, were ten and six. We were awakened by sirens in front of our house unaware of what had happened and taken to neighbors. Early the next morning our mother came into that strange bedroom and gathered her boys around her. I've never forgotten the look on her twenty-eight-year-old face as she told us that our father had been shot and killed.

He was thirty-three years old.

After a few minutes, my brother Joe asked her what was going to happen to us. My mother, Ella Mae Wray, pulled the three of us in tight and said, "I don't know. I don't know what is going to happen to us."

That spring and summer were rough-and-tumble days of protests and movements; and the brutal, violent assassinations of Martin Luther King in April and Robert Kennedy in June. In our black neighborhood within that small town, we all felt the stress, tension, and energy of the times. It was in that climate that my mother had to decide what to do next in her life and for us, her children.

As turbulent as those days seemed, there was also urgency in the air. Change was being encouraged and demanded. It had been a decade and a half since the *Brown v. Board* decision. The Civil Rights Act of 1964 was four years old. It had been two months since her own husband had been gunned down in a small American town when my 28-year-old mother determined what she was going to do for the future of her family. On a mid-summer night in July 1968, Ella Mae Wray once again gathered her three boys and told us of her bold plan: she was going to college.

If this was a difficult plan for a black woman with three small children in 1968, it might have been impossible ten years earlier. After my father's death, realistic options for a young black woman of my mother's working-class circumstances might have been domestic work or a low-level job at the community hospital. But consider what had come in her own lifetime, before the night of her husband's death: not just the Civil Rights

Act and *Brown v. Board*, but also sit-ins, Freedom Summer, marches, court battles, Malcolm, Martin, and four little girls murdered in the struggle. So, a lone black woman's decision to take a bold step was greatly informed and influenced by the political actions and movements of the times and their precursors. The personal was indeed the political.

Let's be clear: Even with years of agitation from Civil Rights, black power movements and rising black women's voices, the Red Sea did not part for my mother, but a space was made. A reluctant sliver, a crack. Just enough for a black woman come north, a widow in an era of famous black widows, a young mother in 1968, to think that college was a possibility and that a college degree might make for a better future for her and her boys. And once she got into that space of opportunity, she fought to increase it, at first by simply being there and eventually by insisting on her right and those of others like her to be there.

My mother being a student at the University of Akron in the late 1960s and early 1970s was eye opening for all of us—her boys, her extended family, and her black small-town Medina community. She exposed us to different challenging ideas, various movement politics and campus fashions. A few years into college she started sporting an afro and my grandmother thought she'd gone mad. But more than anything, my mother's college years helped us to think more broadly about different paths and possibilities that might exist.

In the fall of 1968, on the heels of personal tragedy and national unrest, Ella Mae Wray, a child of the Great Migration, went to college. She changed her life. She changed the lives of her three sons. And she made an impact on her community. In 1968 she was known as Baby Ella after her mother big Ella. By 1972 she was Ella Mae Wray with a BA degree. A few years later she was Professor Ella Mae Wray, MA. By the early 1980s she was Dr. Ella Mae Wray Wilson, vice president of student affairs at Wilberforce University. She passed away in 2000, much too young at sixty-two, but almost every day I think of her as that frightened young widow who started a journey in 1968. Dr. Ella is evidence that the personal is made possible by political and social actions and agitations big and small. That we must fight every day to create space. We must demand it. Then hold it open so that a young black mother with three boys in tow might step into a future that could not possibly be imagined in 1968.

A version of this essay first appeared in The Atlantic, *January 3, 2018, under the title "How Ella Mae Wray Seized the Opportunities of 1968."*

"Orphan District": Segregation in Rural Ohio

JOE BOYLE

Ohio's State Board of Education confronted a dilemma in the fall of 1959. Thirteen miles west of downtown Toledo, Spencer-Sharples Local School District, with a history of poverty and tension dating back nearly a century, had just been split along racial lines. The western, mostly white half of the district seceded to join a more stable neighboring district, leaving the predominantly Black eastern half of the district on its own. As the segregated remainder of Spencer-Sharples struggled to gain state help for their 800 students, State Board of Education member Edward C. Ames penciled a note in the margin of a chart: "Orphan District." It perfectly described Spencer-Sharples; a district without a parent, without a partner, and without equal, one of the ten poorest districts in Ohio. Between 1959 and 1968, the fight for the future of Spencer-Sharples resembled something most Americans would have expected in the Deep South instead of the Upper Midwest.

A History of Division

German immigrants came to Spencer Township first, attracted by fertile land in the north and west. To the south and east was an agriculturally useless mix of sand, swamp, and oak groves—a region referred to as "The Barrens." From the beginning, parallel education systems existed, with four public schoolhouses and one Catholic schoolhouse scattered throughout the township. A series of F4 tornadoes ripped through the region on Palm Sunday of 1920, leveling Catholic and public schools alike, and revealing cultural fault lines. As destructive as the tornadoes were, a township history noted, it "was nothing compared to the community strife which followed."

Catholic families preferred funding a school of their own to a tax hike for public schools. To finance a new public school, supporters of public education needed to create a taxing authority separate from Spencer Township. In late 1920, southeastern Spencer Township seceded and formed a village called Sharples, poaching nearly half of Spencer Township's footprint. Sharples built a school, and after a series of political maneuvers, became Harding Township. The split between Spencer and Harding schools ran counter to a trend of consolidation underway by the 1920s. Between 1900 and 1950, Ohio contracted from 4,000 township school districts to just 446 as small districts merged to create the efficiencies larger districts provide. Separating bore costs for Spencer and Harding; Spencer Township ranked second-to-last in the county for per-pupil funding.

Demographic Change in Spencer Township

During the Great Depression, an enterprising real estate agent dealt off small parcels in "The Barrens" to African Americans from nearby Toledo. It was sold as a way for people just a few years removed from farming in the South to escape the jobless city. But the land wasn't suited to farming, and W. Norton Woods, a member of the Lucas County Board of Education, questioned the motives of the land-dealers:

> Someone discovered that this worthless (I mean worthless) land could be sold for a low price to very poor people who worked in Toledo factories… POOR people moved in, black and white both; but our society being what it is, the decided majority were negro. [Emphasis in original]

"Urban renewal" projects in Toledo drove more African Americans to the area in the 1950s and 1960s. The Black population of Spencer Township jumped from three in 1930 to nearly 4,000 by 1966. As population increased, so did strain on an already-stressed educational system. Three overcrowded schools served elementary students in the two townships, and it was clear they needed to consolidate with neighboring schools.

In 1947, Spencer and Harding townships tried to fold their districts into adjacent Swanton Local Schools. Swanton's board, however, took in only a small swath of Harding Township. Stuck with no one but each other, Spencer and Harding merged to become the Spencer-Sharples Local School District. Primary school students were consolidated at Irwin School, in Spencer Township. Three frame buildings—with open coal furnaces and no plumbing—were built across from Irwin to accommodate the large number of students after consolidation and the influx of Black students. No high school existed, so older students attended Swanton High School on a tuition-basis until 1956, when Swanton refused to take them any longer. The district's children were dispersed among nine area high schools.

Voters in mostly-white western Spencer-Sharples proposed a solution, and in 1959 attempted to dissolve the district, with the west petitioning to join Swanton, and the mostly Black east to petition Springfield. Swanton's board accepted the western parcels, but Springfield voted against absorbing the east. With the west section gone, the unclaimed east remained a Blacker, smaller, and poorer Spencer-Sharples Local School District. The result, U.S. Rep. Lud Ashley noted, was that "school district boundaries were gerrymandered to segregate and contain the area residents, to protect adjacent white areas, and to bring to white areas the prime taxable areas of the original township, while depriving the poor of this resource." The rump district became a 6.75-square-mile district with no meaningful tax base and nearly 1,000 students.

Exceptional Local Control: Orphans and Districts

County and state education boards recognized the problem, but dithered about a solution. County officials favored consolidation, but would "not support the forcing of pupils or territory from one school district upon another [emphasis in original]." The state board began to realize the solution lay outside of their options. For nine years, debate raged over the incompatible goals of consolidating Spencer-Sharples with a nearby district, and the sacrosanct principle of local control. Local control meant that Spencer-Sharples' fate would be decided by a neighboring board, and county officials admitted that the district's "high Negro population ratio will work against any future attempts at consolidation."

With the situation at a stalemate, the Ohio Board of Education faced a secondary dilemma: State policy forbade funding of schools as small as Spencer-Sharples. But a local control rule said "no district maintaining a high school is bound to receive … pupils who live outside the district." In Spencer-Sharples, where every neighboring district refused to accept high school students, the state had to violate one of the contradictory policies. About 120 high school students were in limbo—required to attend school, but with no school to attend. In October, the state authorized a temporary fix, busing the students to a vacant school 17 miles away in Toledo. The state board looked for a way to fund a new high school in Spencer-Sharples, but a board member warned that the state was "condemning the young people of this district to many years of inferior education."

Spencer-Sharples High School opened to great fanfare in 1962, but troubles surfaced quickly. Residents voted themselves the highest property tax rate in the county for maintenance; it generated just $62.95 per year, per student. A new superintendent, William Young, became a lightning rod for many of the district's troubles, which were increasingly seen as part of the larger civil rights movement. In March 1962, the Toledo chapter of the Congress of Racial Equality scheduled a meeting with Young about the conditions at Spencer-Sharples High School— deteriorating in its first year of existence. Irwin was so far beyond repair that the county officials recommended condemnation and demolition. Tensions increased through the year. Young's administration had school board president, Emmett Wheaton, arrested after spending "several hours" at the school talking with teachers and students, and allegedly swearing; he was court-ordered not to set foot on school premises during operating hours. A kindergarten teacher said she had no classroom furniture; she felt "more like a baby sitter than a teacher."

Many understood the complex socioeconomic roots of the problem, but some felt otherwise. In a long letter to state officials, Woods preached citizenship but refused to respect the will of the district's voters. "The County Board will give no help so long as Wheaton[TLW4] is on the SS Board," he wrote. Woods paternalistically suggested that the school's mission must be to teach the community to "follow the rules" because "these adults are mental children." He continued:

> In these days of racial tensions, with NAACP, CORE and governmental agencies, can any white person teach these fundamental precepts of good citizenship without being accused of race prejudice? We of this generation (Caucasians) are not responsible for what happened in the past. Injustices, and lacks that have developed over 100 years can not be corrected in a day, a year, or in ten years; but a start can be made, IF THE NEGROS WILL ACCEPT THE FACTS. [Emphasis in original.]

Caught in the crossfire were the students. In April 1966, the Board fired Young and a third of the teaching staff. A week later, the State Board of Education redoubled its efforts to combine Spencer-Sharples and Springfield. Springfield's board gave no explanation when they rejected the deal, but Schaller told a reporter that Spencer Township's "high Negro population ratio" prohibited consolidation.

Change in Spencer-Sharples

While consolidation appeared dead, major changes approached. An ambitious development plan was formulated by area leaders. In the spring of 1967, county officials briefed business leaders on a plan to create a 700-acre "Oak Openings New Town." It would be a community of about 50,000 people with industrial, residential, and commercial development plotted in concentric bands centered on Spencer-Sharples High School. It was designed to absorb 10,000 central Toledo residents expected to be displaced by redevelopment of "ghettos and blighted neighborhoods." Government and industry coalesced around the plan. Business owners would have fewer obstacles because Spencer Township had federal classification as a "bona fide rural slum," there would be "condemnation powers for acquisition of the ground anyhow." The plan could deliver a windfall in an expanded tax base. Positive change in funding seemed just over the horizon; positive change in leadership was closer.

The district hired a young, new superintendent, Joseph Rutherford, who relished the challenge of learning district administration in such a small setting. From his first days on the job in June, Rutherford learned what a challenge it was. "I got out to Spencer-Sharples... I had a can of keys for the building, and they weren't labeled," Rutherford said. "I couldn't even find a list of who was supposed to be teaching." The three-year-old building "looked like it was 15, 20 years old" Rutherford said. In his first semester, Rutherford ordered testing of the high school pupils to determine a baseline. Only two of the 113 students tested scored above the 50th percentile; thirty scored below the first percentile. When school resumed in fall, Rutherford purchased an American flag for the previously vacant pole. One morning, he received a phone call from a community member who had driven past the school. "She said, 'Joe, your flag's upside down,' and I said 'Hell yes, because we're sinking!'"

Rutherford's arrival, though, signaled that even if the district wasn't sailing smoothly, it at least had stopped taking on water. Rutherford and two board members took a road trip to Alabama in 1967 and recruited four excellent new teachers. A maintenance person was hired. Most importantly, new staffers began to repair relations with the people of Spencer-Sharples by blurring the line between community and school. First year teacher Bill Weber welcomed board members and parents to visit the classroom with or without an appointment. The sense of agency shown in the district between 1966 and 1968 demonstrated that despite Spencer-Sharples' financial situation, good people made a difference under challenging circumstances.

Achieving Consolidation

As the district regained its footing, state and local officials began to examine a way to do something that had never been done in Ohio: Merging Spencer-Sharples with the non-contiguous Toledo Public Schools. The idea appealed to state officials, Rutherford said, because the status quo was "clear *de jure* segregation, and there were lawsuits floating around." More than any other district, Toledo Public could absorb Spencer-Sharples. "If you look around, all those other districts at the time were poor, too. And Toledo was the only district big enough and rich enough," Rutherford said. In June 1967, the Ohio General Assembly passed a narrowly-tailored bill allowing the districts to merge, and six months later, Toledo took over Spencer-Sharples. For Rutherford, it was a moment of relief: "I spent 10 years out there in one 18-month period of time," he quipped. Spencer-Sharples High School and Irwin School remained open after the merger. TPS quickly provided a staff that reflected the community. Flute Rice, a well-regarded district teacher, was installed as the high school principal—the first Black principal in the district's history. Fifteen of the twenty-one teachers assigned to the building were also Black.

Recovery

As a unit of TPS, conditions at Spencer-Sharples improved even beyond the measures taken by Rutherford. A new elementary replaced dilapidated Irwin School. Spencer-Sharples High School adopted a standard curriculum for the first time in its history. The township itself began to change. The first of the 250 public housing units to be built across from the Spencer-Sharples school complex were completed in 1970, along with a community center building full of meeting rooms. A park opened in the middle of the complex. By all appearances, Spencer-Sharples was on the cusp of a new era.

Within five years, however, the New Town withered during a poor national economy. In 1975, after numerous pleas, the federal government pulled all funding for New Town. The aspirations of the community to transcend the generational poverty that had permeated the area since the Great Depression were dashed. With the collapse of the New Town financing, what had been the *raison d'etre* of Toledo Public Schools' takeover of Spencer-Sharples was now officially dead. A 1975 order from the U.S. Department of Health, Education, and Welfare brought some justice—

but planted seeds of destruction. The department ruled that Swanton and Springfield's actions had "resulted in the creation and continued maintenance of a segregated school district." But the department also ruled that the nearly all-Black student body at Spencer-Sharples High School represented illegal segregation. To comply, TPS closed Spencer-Sharples in 1979, and to this day, buses students from the area at least six miles from their homes, across the Springfield district, to integrated schools in Toledo.

2672 South Deacon Street, Detroit

YVONNE

Rickety wood box of a house
Two stories with a pitched roof
White bottom, black top, peeling
Paint, straight out flat the shipping
Crate, set right up on hard bare ground.
(No disrespect) in strange Berlin.

Why? Some mover opened these doors.
Some shaker trod these floors,
Traced these stairs, leaned against these walls
(Never in despair?) from hours
Hunting a bit of work. Life trickles
On. With or without a name.

Montgomery, Hampton, Detroit—even fame
Traveled on, after fingerprints, bail, no job—strife
Unearned, hate mail, threats—after boycott there's life
Pulled/pushed, never untouched, she found herself,
Hubby by her side, at brother's door.
This same door—not ramshackle then. Poor.

"Home is where they have to take you in."
How many children underfoot? Fifteen!
A little peace with those who knew her when.
Recipes by heart. Griddle cakes, apple butter.
Chicken with dumplings, blueberry cobbler.
Piece work in the basement. Two years. Then gone.

Some say death comes in threes. Then a fourth.
Children birth themselves and leave the hearth.
Simple things. Despite a fabled kinswoman.

Did she ever own? Not even this
One precious home? Put under glass.
This refugee, of a sort. This haven.

The house of Sylvester McCauley, Jr., the sole sibling of Rosa Parks, had been lost to foreclosure when his daughter, Rhea McCauley, saved it from demolition for $500 in 2008. After many efforts to have it restored, she partnered with the artist Ryan Mendoza to ship it to his Berlin backyard where he re-assembled it. At this writing it has been returned to the USA where it sits in the storage facility of Guernsey's Auction.

This piece was first published in the online journal Poets Reading the News *in February 2019.*

"Tell 'Em What We Did!": Choosing and Building Black Space in the Midwest

MICHELLE S. JOHNSON

When I reiterate the value of Black spaces, I often search stunned faces and remind myself I was granted lines of cultural ancestry through two fathers, Roy S. Merricks in Kalamazoo, Michigan and Albert D. Johnson in Saginaw, Michigan. I descend from Black bartenders, performers, cooks, construction workers, drivers, and beauticians who lived, worked, visited or ran businesses and homes near commercial and residential neighborhoods along the Saginaw and Kalamazoo Rivers. My folks worked alongside the reigning paper and automobile industries and rooted me in stories that elevated residential, social, political, and commercial life in the Black Midwest. They refused to relegate the powerful lessons of Black autonomy to times past or the lost spaces of Tulsa's distant Midwest edge, Chicago's Bronzeville, Detroit's Black Bottom and Paradise Valley, or the Ville in St. Louis. The Merricks, Woods, Chaneys, Davises, Mathewses of Kalamazoo, the Johnsons of Saginaw, and their communities, challenge a singular perspective that erases, ignores, or simply doesn't know the instructive layers that Black Michiganders generated in well-known places and smaller, impactful places like Saginaw and Kalamazoo as they co-created sustaining residential, political, educational, entertainment and, economic models.

The people who held down Black space speak up loudly and clearly while instructing me to "Tell 'Em What We Did!"* As a Hurstonian scholar, I have dedicated most of my career to listening to individuals in my family and other narrators who demonstrate first-hand accounts of historical, personal, and ancestral insistence on shaping spaces. Like author

---

*As I questioned my motivation to complete this essay in the last days of the decade of one of my most impactful years, gazing outside or inside my head yielded nothing. Finally, in rising from a backward stretch across my yoga ball, I saw two four-story high blended pines in the next block. As I contemplated how these two trees came to share such intimate space and nearly equal height, I heard a message that said "Tell 'em what we did!" Pictures and family "artifacts" fill and inspirit the area on and around the green and brown metal trunk I re-conditioned over 20 years ago, but I have never received such an indistinguishably loud or unified message. And thus, the essay and its title appear here.

and anthropologist Zora Neale Hurston, I am informed by and dedicated to showing the cultural roots of Black insistence and how Black people in places like Kalamazoo and Saginaw built and sustained vital and interconnected spaces. They accomplished this by generating and maintaining business hubs, buying and managing urban property, retaining "country" living by purchasing rural land and buildings, and helping to fuel several Black resorts in Michigan.

My father and godfather in Kalamazoo married a woman whose family came to Southwest Michigan from North Carolina in the first nineteenth-century wave of Black migration between 1830 and 1860. My grandparents and thousands of individuals and configurations of Black people migrated to Kalamazoo and Saginaw in the later two waves of movement that characterized larger cities like Detroit or Chicago between 1910 and 1970. My grandparents left behind the restrictions of Mississippi and Louisiana with insistence on a life just a little less tenuous. At age fifteen, my Grandma Woods left Natchez, Mississippi, either with a newborn or to bear my father in Kansas City, before coming to Kalamazoo around 1920.

Before my grandmother was born, her parents lived on the farm my great-grandfather rented and worked near Natchez with two children. By the time she was nine in 1910, she had five siblings and her father worked on one of the Mississippi River's abundant steamboats while my great grandmother worked as a cook for a private family. In Kalamazoo, Black laborers, porters, domestics, laundresses, cooks, and waiters worked for private families and businesses. They boosted Black presence in the area and placed the city with the second highest number of Black residents in the state, though far behind Detroit. When my grandmother settled in Kalamazoo's Northside River Community in the 1920s, she, like her mother, cooked for hotels and private families and, at the time of her death, an Eastside Country Club. Boarders and heads of households settled the Northside "Bottoms" west of the Kalamazoo River and north of downtown, and by the 1930s, found homes in and around the floodplain east of the river.

As Black families moved north, they retained and modified models from their southern origins and created homes that served the needs of family, community and economic autonomy. Some Black people purchased and/or maintained homes that generated income by boarding long and short-term residents new to town or desiring the benefits of home without the full financial, dietary, and household responsibilities. In Saginaw as early as the '50s, "hotbed" room rentals sometimes coincided with the shifts of the twenty-four-hour-a-day production at Malleable or Grey Iron Plant and, in a maximization of space and economy, men rented rooms during 7am-3pm, 3pm-11pm or 11pm-7am slots.

Like other Black people in the Midwest, my grandparents' large homes, established on Black land or in Black neighborhoods, created hubs of family nurturance and sustained integral cultural elements through networks of stories, news, commentary, economic exchange, and recreation. My Grandma Chaney-Woods used her home in Kalamazoo to raise my father in the 1920s and early '30s and allotted rooms for her brothers and sisters who followed from Natchez, until later renting two long-term rooms to quiet musicians and bartending men like my father until her death.

My grandmother, Gertrude Earl Johnson, was born in Taylor County, Florida on family land about fifty crow's miles from Rosewood, the site of the 1923 massacre. Along with her brother, she retained the Florida land and inherited agricultural property and a home in Cottonport, Louisiana. In 1951, my grandparents and their ten children left the Cottonport farmhouse that burned during an unexplained fire where my grandfather, Oscar Johnson, and Uncle Cariton climbed the two-story building to break windows and narrowly rescued my grandmother and the newborn twins. While my grandmother kept her share of family property in Louisiana, my grandparents purchased their homes and property in Carrolton and Saginaw, though no one ever returned to farm or live.

Having followed my grandmother's brother to Carrollton after purchasing land and a home for the nine Johnson children aged newborn to seventeen years old, my grandparents continued rural living and grew some of the family food while some sons took jobs at the GM plant. Dirt roads, back gardens, shotgun houses, and fields grounded my Johnson dad and remained a life anchor as he hunted, fished and initiated country rides and farm-stand visits. After my grandfather's traumatic death on a construction site in 1963, my grandmother maintained a "country" place in bordering Buena Vista where my aunts and their families periodically lived. She purchased the homes she lived in after my grandfather's untimely death.

Black urban life in Saginaw in the '50s and '60s boomed in the Potter Street district and roared across the 6th Street Bridge from Carrollton and south side of the Saginaw River. My Aunt Mammie (pronounced May-me) Jones, who had been coming there with my family since they moved from Cottonport, held down a beauty shop from 1964-1991 behind Barbara's, a woman-owned barber shop on 6th Street near Farwell (pronounced Fare-well). Along this commercial corridor, shot-gun style buildings contained prominent commercial and residential life where the multifaceted community generated business and social structures while plant laborers melted iron and poured it into mold castings for engine blocks. Here, Black people owned and frequented twenty-four hour soul food restaurants, grocery stores, a tailor shop, barber and beauty shops, a drug store, a fish market, ice cream parlors, cleaner and a pool hall, a beer garden, dance hall, bars and a recreation establishment deemed a "baby casino" by my Uncle Rollie. Black business people like Arthur Braggs, Leodell Braggs, and Memphis Pete and their staff circulated and maintained intricate bookmaking networks in local Black homes, shops and social spaces. Working across the state in places like Lansing and Detroit, notable entrepreneur, Braggs, spread the financial benefits of the system through multiple businesses, including the entertainment leader, Idlewild Revue, a Saginaw skating rink, the Hickory House restaurant and regular youth-centered block parties that provided free refreshments and activities.

Through layered, complicated and sometimes dramatic relationships, I emerged in 1962 and, over my formative years, landed in three illustrative Black communities, a hundred years or more in the making. Then Susan R. Tyo, my twenty-year-old mother and white Western Michigan University student, met my forty-five-year-old father as he worked maintenance for the university. They dated in racially accepting spaces like Battle Creek's black and tan nightclub, Bellman and Porters, the Eastside Pacific Club (PI) or smaller venues like the Elk's Lodge where my mom waitressed before conceiving me and moving to our North Avenue home. My Kalamazoo father, Roy, didn't insist on inhabiting white space, instead, he rooted us in culturally specific Black communities where my mother, not he, integrated. In the course of his life, this father navigated the world as a professional drummer and sometime bass player in Kalamazoo and Grand Rapids, a cook during the Korean War, a bartender in Chicago and Kalamazoo, and a New York cab driver turned hearse driver for a Kalamazoo funeral home. In his late forties, my father's income balanced between a long-standing tradition of Black mixologists and the occasional local gig.

As I entered the world, we lived in the opposite unit of a North Avenue duplex that we shared with the couple next door, the leader of my father's band, King Oliver and His Men, and his wife. One of several like it, our building sat along one of the main thoroughfares of what newspapers and officials of the time called the "ghetto." My first, but nowhere near my last, time living in a neighborhood deemed pathology at one of the heights of its power, I absorbed the strength of syncopation, bass and improvisation as the thin walls of this shotgun home allowed after-hours jam sessions with the band and, for me, nestled in a dresser drawer, muted jazz lullabies that still soothe me. Our pulsing house sat the next block east of Kalamazoo's economic boycott victory against racial discrimination at Van Avery Drug Store in 1963 and a little under a mile past the Black residential hub of the "Bottoms" along Walbridge and across the river from another long-standing Eastside settlement of Black people in the Riverview area.

As was often the case in Michigan hubs of Blackness, the Kalamazoo community sustained entertainment venues that built and maintained community. In 1946, on the Eastside, my oldest sister's mom, Emma Davis, helped establish the books before managing the front of the house for the Black-owned high-end Pacific or "PI" Club. Founder Council Hawes anchored the growing population in the Eastside neighborhood and intentionally promoted civil rights with his integrated venue. The club provided a bottle club for members' personal liquor and set-ups to accompany entertainment, quality food, innovative and "classy" presentation and the venue's own tableware.

Through an abrupt turn of events, my parents moved to Chicago and I came to consciousness on or near Stony Island between Jackson Park and 75th, a strip of buildings housing my preschool, and the bar where my dad worked during a recognition and amplification of Black power. Our building at 69th and Stony held multiple apartments above Red's Bar where we shared a bathroom with other tenants as our flat faced the activity of a Southside center where Blackstone Rangers and Rangerettes congregated in an environment of a renewed expression of radicalism: the presence of the Nation of Islam, and Cassius Clay becoming Muhammad Ali passing out the *Final Call* and hanging out around the corner at a local garage. My parents balanced my care between my mother's day-schedule as an operator for Bell Telephone in Chicago, my father's nighttime bartending shifts, and the rigorous preschool owned and operated by a Black woman.

My parents balanced the congested, loud and fast-moving environment with occasional trips to places with serene land and water as we visited Paradise Lake, a 185-acre body of water and one of five Black resorts in Michigan. Black visitors helped make up a forty-decade flow of people who owned or leased large and midsize homes while others rented cabins or rooms at the elaborate Gray Hotel. Black people established this and other retreat venues as destinations in Cass, Van Buren, and St. Joseph Counties especially for Chicagoans, Detroiters, and Black people from across the state who rented and owned vacation property where they fished, swam, conversed, and relaxed. The mother of all resorts, Idlewild, overshadowed these smaller settings including nearby Woodland Park, where later Louise Little, Malcolm X's mother, lived her last twenty-six years after a previous twenty-six-year incarceration in the Kalamazoo State Hospital.

In 1967, my mother and I moved to a small one-bedroom apartment in a hostile, white and predominately second- or third-generation German and Polish neighborhood, directly across from the twenty-four-hour soot spewing Steering Gear plant on Salt Street on Saginaw's southwest side. Soon after, she married my Saginaw father, A.D. Johnson. Just months from moving from Chicago, I learned Saginaw race relations and where I was most safe. In July, the mayor and police thwarted legitimate requests for recreational spaces for Black youth and antagonized, attacked, and patrolled formerly peaceful protesters, forcing Black people across the four bridges connecting the two side, shutting down the bridges, and wounding seven people at 6th and Lapeer street. Through insistent acts all over the Eastside and at the nascent Delta Community College miles away from town, Black activists and protesters like my Aunt Betty Hassan rallied and insisted that businesses, politicians and police see and address their concerns, some issuing speeches, some disrupting property and others setting things afire. As my family navigated the shut-down, the bridge to reunite us in my grandmother's 22nd and Lapeer Eastside home, protest shouts and gunshots punctuated the ether outside. I, not yet five, learned to crouch to avoid angered Black or oppressive police-directed bullets, while learning the tenuous safety of family as my 6'7 dad stood century, rifle in hand prepared to shoot anyone who threatened us.

As in substantive Black neighborhoods across the country and Flint, Detroit and Lansing, Saginaw officials and developers implemented policies that tattered communities at their height of power. In 1968, just a year after racial uprisings in Saginaw, the city allowed the highway, which we knew was intended to be wide enough for tanks if revolt occurred again, to run through one of our central Black neighborhoods. My Aunty Betty and Uncle Ahmad, the family revolutionaries, lost their home as construction began for the four-lane I-675 highway just outside their door. Despite courtroom protests and occasional stubborn hold-outs, federal and local government officials exacted "urban renewal" as an aggressive and unfair process of taking Black homes, often demolishing them and intentionally dismantling central Black hubs across town. 6th Street began a slow decline.

On 6th in Saginaw today, Mt Olive Baptist and a parking lot for the congregants now inhabit the land of my youth and young adulthood. These buildings stood vacant for years after 1986 when GM's divestment in Saginaw glared apparent and businesses closed. As the industry took the jobs and left the environmental footprint of vacancy and toxicity, the buildings aged, were demolished, and the land bank picked up the property until Mt. Olive, a dedicated resident since 1941, acquired the land.

In Kalamazoo, local white activists fought the introduction of a bypass that would have disrupted downtown in the early '80s, but the former "Bottoms" smacks of White "reinvasion," as life-long Tennessee civil rights activist Leo Lillard calls gentrification. After decades of divestment by the city and, some would argue, its black community, hastily built and meanly managed apartments inhabit the Walbridge strip where Black men and women residents, then artist hipsters, rooted their communities. Black Northside and Eastside leadership has not ceded the communities to a narrative of pathology or abandonment as Mattie Jordan-Woods and Pat Taylor organize and leverage their personal and professional power as Executive Directors of impactful neighborhood associations.

Most of the people who nurtured me since my childhood are gone. Grief is all too present. Yet, these folks of mine are strong-willed and intend to ensure a cultural presence in the future. They want others to know what they did. Watching their brilliant accomplishments and near erasures, I heed these urges to garner the lessons of our pasts by documenting, strengthening, and generating centers of Black autonomy and authenticity. I am, after all, the child of a pantheon of space makers and I sometimes listen.

The Great Migration of African-American Southerners to Cleveland: "From Down South Up South"

EDITED BY EDWARD M. MIGGINS

The Great Migration of approximately eight million African-American Southerners to the USA's North, Midwest, and the West occurred between the end of Reconstruction in 1877 and 1980. They escaped the South's Jim Crow-society that attempted to re-establish racial apartheid through violence, disenfranchisement, unequal and non-existent schools, segregation, sharecropping, poverty and inequality. Black Southerners began to see opportunities in industrial cities, particularly during the labor shortages during WWI and WWII, as a Promised Land: Better paying jobs, schools and housing and greater respect for their civil liberties and right to vote. Southern Blacks who worked as sharecroppers could be employed, for the first time, as wage workers. By 1920, 40% of the nation's black population lived in eight cities, including five in the Midwest: New York, Philadelphia, Pittsburgh, Chicago, Detroit, Cincinnati, Columbus, and Cleveland. They could see with pride the establishment of black-controlled neighborhoods, businesses, newspapers, churches, fraternal associations, civil rights and social service organizations, women's clubs, and entertainment as a successful foothold in urban America. On the other hand, black residents faced discrimination in employment, housing, public recreation and personal relationships that denied their civil rights and racial equality. W. E. B. Dubois, the first black graduate of Harvard and one of the founders of the NAACP (1911), believed that African-Americans would discover themselves and their freedom by resisting racial oppression, as you can learn from following interview excerpts. By 1960, approximately 250,000 African-Americans lived in Cleveland—30% of the city's population—primarily as a result of the Great Migration.

"It turned into a new world": Bertha Cowen (St. J.)*

"The Negroes were leaving the South, because there was a better world for them… White folks didn't know too much about the Negroes in the North. This is when the South all came up here and it turned into a new world."

Bertha Cowen migrated from Lynchburg, Virginia in 1917.

"From Down South Up South": Rev. L. F. Hill (St. J.)

"I remember when John Hay High School, at Carnegie and E. 107th, first opened up, it was a business high school where you learned to do secretarial work and it was very difficult for a Negro to get in that school. They just didn't want them in there. Let me tell you this about Cleveland. My daddy brought me from down South up North. But, after I became older and became a man, I found out that he really brought me from down South up South. Because in Cleveland, when I grew up, colored people could not eat in restaurants downtown. They could not use the facilities of the hotels downtown. In the five-and-ten-cent store, they could not sit down at the counter to eat. They could only stand up to eat."

In 1917, Rev. Hill migrated from Washington, D.C. when he was 6 or 7 years old. His family originated in Virginia.

"Don't let nothing bug you!": Elmer B. Thompson (CHP)

"My name is Elmer B. Thompson. I was born in Indianapolis, Indiana on July 22, 1895. My father was born as a slave on a blue ribbon horse farm in Kentucky… After emancipation, he moved to Cincinnati; his grandmother was there. When we came to Cleveland (1901), my father worked for an asphalt company… When we moved here, I was just old enough to go to school; I was six years old. Cleveland was like a foreign country-everybody was speaking Jewish or Italian or whatever. The neighborhoods colored people lived in were the same neighborhoods that the other people who came lived in. I went to Marion School and on a Jewish holiday there were twelve of us in school—five Blacks out of 40. There were two Catholic boys that didn't like to be whipped in the Catholic schools… I decided not to go to college and I took the course they called shop at East Tech…When I went to high school, my parents never bought one pencil for me and I contributed a little while I was going to school; they needed it… I was the first one in my family to get a high school graduation diploma… One teacher would always say that nobody would hire a Black for electrical work. I finally told him one day that I won't ask anybody to hire me-and I haven't so far. After I graduated, I went to work for myself. I was fortunate; people were burning gas lights and wanted to convert to electricity. During my last year in school, I was doing a little electric work... I'd go up in the hottest attic there is on the Fourth of July if I got paid for it. I couldn't get into the union, because my face was Black. That's the only reason. I was all that time on talking terms with them from 1915. I was doing a building, a store on Kinsman and the union came in there. I'd saw the white plumber run and jump out the back window upstairs where there was going to be a porch onto a pile of stuff. I didn't know what the devil he was running for. It turns out the plumber was non-union labor. They said, 'You got a card?' I said, 'Sure'. I pulled out "Thompson and West Electric Construction," not a union card. I didn't know about the union card. He said, 'No, a union card.' I said, 'Union card, where can I get one?' I always was able to out-talk the union men. I'd say, 'Well, to tell you the truth, if I was getting the same money you're getting, I would be doing the same thing you're doing. But, I wasn't born in Slovakia or no place like that, I was born here in the United States; I'm a native-born American citizen. Now, whatever you do to me, you're doing it against a native-born American citizen. So, as far as I'm concerned, this is my job, and I'll tell you what you better do. (I'd pull my hat down.) You'd better get the hell on off of here, you understand? Do you know what I'm talking about?' And they would be gone. But then I'd have to ease back and watch that job, go there and stay till dark to see if they were going to come to clip the wires because they clipped five houses on me once and they cut them so slick. If you cut it where it's tied around a knob, you could cut it and it would look like it's still there. You got to go in and snap each wire and see if it works loose to see if it's cut. But, I didn't let it bother me. I was born with a thing that says, 'Don't let nothing bug you!' And that's the way I've lived all my life."

Elmer B. Thompson migrated from Indianapolis when he was 6 years old in 1901. His family originated from Kentucky.

"We always laughed at those peckerwoods": Murtis Taylor (St. J.)
"The first place I went to apply for a job and got it was May Company. I went to the May Company and was working in the stockroom and the woman who had charge came to me and said, 'You know, you're doing so well in the stockroom, I really want to put you in the French Room.' The French Room was where they sold French hats and French Dresses; it was very exclusive. I would have made more money in the French Room. I can't remember the

name of this Black person, who was passing for white, in the French Room, but she was passing and she was a salesperson in the French Room. On Monday, I was supposed to be in the French Room. Well, I went there and I sat down and I'm grinning, because I'm so glad I'm going to the French Room. Her expression had changed entirely and she said 'I'm sorry, we know some things about you we did not know when we hired you. Your services are no longer needed. So, I looked in the paper and I saw this job that said they needed waitresses at the RC Sandwich Shop. So, I went down and I applied and I got it. They had horseshoe counters; that's where you served the people. So, I was getting along all right there. One day, sitting at my counter came these two women, light brown. Mr. and Mrs. Crosby owned this place. Mr. Crosby kept walking up and down and looked at these women. He made up his mind that they were colored and he went to the block boy. The block boy was the one who prepared the sandwiches. He said to the block boy, 'They're colored; you know what to do.' So, what he did was to fill their sandwiches so full of salt that they couldn't eat it. This was what restaurants did during this period. They brought their sandwiches, they took one bite and they couldn't eat it. In here, I'm feeling all nervous. What shall I do? I need this job. They couldn't eat it. They left their sandwich and they went to pay. Mr. Crosby came up and said, 'You don't need to pay, because we don't want your patronage.' Then he went to the table and took those plates and broke them over the counter. I never did tell him I was colored, but I came home and cried every night. I said, 'I need the job, I won't be able to go South. My mother won't have the money and my father won't have the money to go South.' This was a terrible ordeal. Mrs. Crosby really liked me. She came in one day. She had been on the streetcar. They didn't have buses in those days. She said, 'Oh, I'm so upset, Murtis.' I said: 'What happened?' She said: 'A nigger came and sat next to me on the streetcar. You couldn't tell at first that this was a nigger. Do you know how to tell a nigger?' I said: 'No, how do you tell a nigger?' She said: 'If they have white marks on their fingernails, you know they are colored.' She said: 'Didn't you know that?' I said, 'No, ma'am.' But I stayed there. I got good tips and some of the whites would invite me to their parties. All the whites working there lived on the west side. And I questioned whether I should go down to these parties. Well, there was a family here called the Tudor Family; they were very fair. So I would invite Bill Tudor to go and we always laughed at these peckerwoods, because we were really putting something over on them. Now, that family was very fair, and they all went west and passed for white. They're still out there passing for white."

Murtis H. Taylor migrated from Brunswick, Georgia. She was born in Macon, Georgia in 1911.

"We just can't get rid of this guy... I got the job": Sammie Mays (CEM)

"I saw there weren't any Blacks in the electrical department. They said to take a test. The first test I made seven hundred; you had to get at least six-hundred-fifty out of a thousand. They said when an opening comes, you can have it. I said it's an opening on the board. So, I went back for the same job again. The man said I had to take a test. I said I already took a test. He said, 'You didn't take a test.' I said, 'I did take the test.' So, he said, 'Well, you've got to take another one.' I took the test, but this time I made nine hundred fifty. So the guy told the supervisor, 'Hell, he made more this time than he did before. We just can't get rid of that guy.' So the super said, 'Why do you want this job? You just want it because there aren't any Black guys on it.' I said, 'Naw, I want it because you make more money.' At that time, I was only making $3 an hour. The guys on the electric department were making $7.50 an hour. I said, 'That's where I want to go. They make $4.50 more than I do. So, that's why I want to get on the job.' He said, 'I believe you'd take my job, wouldn't you?' I said, 'Sure, I would take your job. I can handle your job. All I've got to do is go sit in the office and tell them, 'Don't hire any Black people. That's all your job consists of. Keep the Black people out and bring Japanese and Germans in. The ones we were fighting.' Then, I got the job. I stayed on that job, then I ended up being an electrical foreman."

Sammie Mays was born in Macon, Georgia in 1946 and migrated the same year. (CEM)

"I didn't know colored people played the violin": Weltha Lilly (CCC)

"I worked in one of my girlfriend's places. She was housecleaning and got sick. This woman was going to have a party and she had promised faithfully to be there. She asked me to go in her place. I went there and cleaned up the lady's house. She told me to put some stuff away she wanted to stick away in her closets, because she was going to have company. There was a violin. I said, 'Oh, you play the violin?' She said, 'I used to.' I said, 'So did I.' And she said to me—these are little things in my life that show me the misconceptions of white people about colored people—'Oh, I didn't know colored people played violins.' I looked at her and I guess my expression must have been that I thought she was crazy. I came home and told my mother about it and my mother laughed. And she said, 'Poor dear.' That's what Mama said. That was all. To me, it first made me think how ignorant they were. Next I wanted to know where'd they get it from? So that's how I got involved in Black history from my knowledge of why people thought that way that I couldn't understand."

Weltha Lilly was born in Cleveland in 1914. Her father came from Cook County, Georgia. (CHP)

"Everything was peaches and cream": Ella May Sharpe (St. J.)

"I met my lifelong friend, Jane Logan, there at that school. Now, this principal would not let us eat in the lunchroom. Fortunately, Loretta White's father was the head of the Urban League operating down on 40th Street. He came down to the school and found out that not only she was doing this to us, but she was having the whites wash in one basin and the blacks in another. And when he found out about that, she went from room to room. I don't know what kind of language he used. But she reversed that and said, 'Children, since you are not fighting like you used to, we can all wash in the same basin now. We can all come in the same door'… And so everything was peaches and cream."

Ella May Sharpe migrated from Atlanta to Cleveland during the WWI era and became a public-school teacher in Cleveland. (CHP)

"No more trouble with him at all": Effie Watkins (CHP)

"I remember that one Italian boy's father was a wine maker. He had a big wine mill. We was living on railroad tracks, and them boxcars of grapes would come in down there for him. This one boy was around my age, but he was stouter than me. And my brother was five years old then. My brother had to always wait for me when we would get out of school. Wickliffe School set up on a little hill and we had to come down the steps and we wasn't supposed to break rank until we got out on the street. So my brother was standing out there waiting for me and this boy. Just as I come out of class coming out of the building, he pulled my brother's hat off and hit my brother. Then he looked up and seen me and he started around back of the building. I then cut class. I cut out of the line and he went around the back-and we had swings in the back. I caught him around there with those swings and I beat him good. (laughter) Well, (laughter) he made friends… So, when his father's boxcars came in with the grapes, he would give us whole boxes of grapes out of his father's grapes (laughter). I had no more trouble with him at all. I give him a good whopping. I had to go to the principal, and Mrs. Moore went right along with me (laughter) and said, 'Effie had to protect him.' (laughter) So that is one woman that inspired me in life, that really took up for me and helped me a lot."

In 1901, Effie Watkins was born in Humburg, Tennessee and migrated in 1917.

"Maybe that was good for me": Dorothy Layne McIntyre (CCC)

"When I saw Dorothy (her white friend with an identical first name), I said, 'Dorothy, I understand they made a mistake when they told me (my essay) was the best in the class. They said it was your paper." She said. 'It was.' She said, 'All I know is the principal called me down to her office and said, 'Let us correct your paper, so we can send it in.' That was not a mistake. The principal helped me rewrite it so it could be sent in, Dorothy.' I said, 'Well, there you go.' That was my first experience, of many experiences, and it made me a little leery with prejudices, with that type of discrimination. I was deflated, but I bounced back. Then, from that time on, I said, 'I bet you one thing. I bet very few white students will be ahead of me scholastically.' And I stayed up all the way through. Maybe that was good for me, to keep on pushing."

Dorothy Layne McIntyre was born in Leroy, New York in 1917 and migrated to Cleveland in 1940. Her family came from Virginia. After serving as a pilot in the USA's Civilian Air Corps, she became a public-school teacher in Cleveland.

*These are excerpts of transcripts from Cuyahoga Community College's Oral History and Community Studies Center that contain oral histories on the Great Migration from Cuyahoga Community College (CCC), Cleveland Ethnographic Museum (CEM), St. James AME Church (St. J.), and Cleveland Public Library's Cleveland Heritage Program (CHP). They will be incorporated into *Voices of the Great Migration of African-American Southerners to Cleveland: 'A Community of Memory' through Oral and Social History* and Vol. I and II *of The Great Migration of Southern African-Americans to Cleveland: Journey to 'Hope City', 1619-2019"* edited by Edward M. Miggins and produced by Cleveland State University's Engaged Scholarship Program. Edward M. Miggins attended Fairfield, Case Western Reserve and Columbia Universities. You can contact him at edmiggins@gmail.com

the negro in minneapolis (for prince & philando castile)

brian g. gilmore

that time i drove to minneapolis from
east lansing to read stories w/ some black
people & ate nicoise salads
saw dozens of somalians who
stood outside in the cold &
kicked a soccer ball all day &
smoked cheap american cigarettes
that clouded their spaces like in card
games or bowling alleys in the old
days when life was simple   AM radio
black & white television   hot
dogs boiled & eaten w/ mustard
george mikan shooting hookshots
for the lakers

the city recalled that time or maybe it
was st paul   the other
of the twins   where f scott
learned how to gatsby but also
why he had to leave & go in search
of his soul   or maybe it was a
black woman poet who loved to dance
as if dancing was writing haiku   & so
she threw a party for a prince who lived in
the city   the same prince who zoomed
to life not long after the days of boiled
hot dogs w/ mustard   AM radio was dying
& people smoked cheap cigarettes in
bowling alleys

missed that party but so many came to write haiku
that evening   no one had space to write anything
they just danced & clapped their hands & partied
like it was the end of days   somalians ruled my
evening insteadsomething about men darker than
chunks of coal kicking around a soccer ball w/ not
a care in the world in one of the coldest places is
reassuring   like on airplane flights & they
begin serving mixed drinks at 38,000 feet

only other thing i did in minneapolis besides poems & stories
& somalians is jog in the snow   flurries floated around
me like confetti   like when mikan's lakers won it all & they
were champagne drinking happy   it was a wondrous time
did not even know then that dred scott once lived here as a
slave long before roger taney declared him nothing   but
lester young blew horn on the north side here in the '20s in his father's
band & gordon parks played blues piano in some brothel downtown
before he made magic w/ those cameras

& the prince of this city who zoomed to life was still alive dreaming
& writing songs & throwing parties that lasted forever   philando
castille had not yet reached for his wallet & then all those cameras
& marchers & tweeters came running to talk about it like joe
kapp running for a first down across an ice rink of a football field to
try again to win it all for the locals

Realizing Freedom

PHYLLIS M. MAY-MACHUNDA

Driven to make real
    illusive dreams of freedom,
my ancestors forsook Southern plantations to establish homes
     in the Union-supporting Midwest.
Seizing long awaited opportunities
    they caravanned North and West to Southern Illinois,
    crossing the Jordan into Little Egypt,
     to acquire, toil, and forge their fate on "their own pieces of land"
     at the nexus of the Big Muddy & Ohio Rivers.
Consecrating liberation.
Realizing freedom!
Donning the armor of God, these freed men and women fashioned
    kin and friends-based networks of burgeoning communities
    nestled in Southern sympathizer territory,
    around earthen Indian mounds of prior Native dwellers.
 They raised devoutly prayerful churches with lined out hymns and sparsely
furnished schools
     open to all seekers of faith, literacy, and ciphering, regardless of age,
    to learn to read, write, figure, play, and "walk in the way."
Interdependent on trust, integrity and allies for business and survival,
    they adamantly demonstrated the humanity requisite of good citizenship
    as they labored communally and in hopeful self-reliance.
Enacting liberation.
Realizing freedom!
Vigilant freedmen, grateful for less daily precarity,
    tilled linear designs in the fertile loam of the Ohio with plows and mules
    planting, then harvesting corn, sorghum, peanuts, and beans
    raising, then butchering a cow, some chickens, and curing a couple of hogs
     while dependent on bounteous woods and streams to fill out family
meals and
simultaneously laboring as sawyers, carpenters, blacksmiths, masons, cooks,
    pastors, railroadmen, undertakers, and businessmen to attend to family
and community needs.

Embracing liberation.

Realizing freedom!

Organizing women, the heart and pulse of their village communities,

   toiling as laundresses, housekeepers, seamstresses, teachers, and caretakers for others,

      buttressed their own homes as shelters for those they held dear and pieced together fractured families as patchwork quilts.

      Nursing daily indignities with salves of possibilities and respect, polishing children so their manners, lessons, and appearance shone,

         gathering eggs, nuts, berries, and Earth's abundance as the seasons changed,

      they sculpted out spare moments to tend their own cherished blooming and edible gardens,

      then dried, cooked, and canned delectable products in their care.

Embodying liberation.

Real-izing freedom!

In realizing, embodying, embracing, enacting, and modeling freedom, my emancipated ancestors planted and fortified footings for

   seven Midwestern generations since

   to continue the quests of actualizing and maintaining our liberation despite

      confronting intermittent but persistent resistance to our full humanity.

III.
LOVE

There is always something left to love. And if you ain't leaned that, you ain't learned nothing.
—Lorraine Hansberry

(Born in Chicago, Illinois, 1930)

No One Loves me, Like I love Me

KATHERINE SIMÓNE REYNOLDS

"The love I gained with such uphill effort and self-defacement was not meant for me at all but for the me I created to please them"—Alice Miller

I created this series out of a need to see something emotional at a very hectic and lonely time in my life. I didn't tell the subject, Demetre, what the concept of the shoot was because I didn't have one. I had a need to make something that was raw and bright. Something that was colorful and Queer, yet still had a sense of abandonment. With a rented pink suit, and an uncontrollable need to work, I used this shoot like a diary entry.

No One Loves me, like I love Me is meant to have the "bad grammar" with certain "loves" and "Me's having capital letters to set the juxtaposition between self love/self deprecation. This series is on the cusp of forlorn and celebration.

Katherine (Kat) Simóne Reynolds
theunsuspended.com

Stay Debaucherous

DAVID WEATHERSBY

It was freezing, absolutely freezing. This was to be expected for mid-December in Chicago, but still, it was freezing. It was my third time around the same block as I searched for the deliberately covert address that I had just received four hours earlier. This was by design. It was a clever way of quite literally keeping the creeps away. This wasn't my first time at this event but it was my first time since it had gained somewhat of a reputation. On my fourth pass, I was starting to wonder if there was going to be an event at all. I did notice a modest crowd starting to form around an unmarked door. I was desperate for any sign that I hadn't fallen victim to a massive GPS error, so I slowed down to see if the crowd would grow. I noticed more cars slowly pulling up to the location, each one pausing in front of this unmarked door, seemingly waiting for some sign of confirmation just as I was.

I was confident enough at this point to park in the spot I had magically found and been idling in for twenty minutes. I was ready to brace the cold wind that was waiting for me outside of the car door. I had been a videographer in Chicago for some time at this point so late nights and run and gun setups were a norm for me. With a combination of preparation and a bit of good fortune, I would get the footage I needed. This was years before I was producing documentaries, so I was not there for any ethnographical research adventure. I was simply asked to shoot the event by my friend Khari and it was as much a fulfillment of curiosity as it was a video shoot. He had started the event as a way to celebrate his birthday and I knew three things about it: it was secretive, they played house music, and it was called Thee Debauchery Ball.

As I gathered my equipment and started for the door, I noticed that knee-to-ankle-length coats were popular amongst the crowd waiting to get in. It was understandable due to the evening weather, but there was a sense of something clandestine in the air. We entered the elevator and rode up together with a low murmur of small talk until we arrived at our floor. As the doors opened, we rounded the corner into a typical office and studio building. We could feel the music before we heard it as the distant volume seemed to slowly rise in the room. The crowd around me began to shed their heavy coats, hats and gloves revealing an array of black, erotic clothing that ran the gamut from night-out sexy black dresses to body paint and very little (if anything) else.

We came to a table at the entrance of the last door in the hall. The woman at the table saw the camera in my hand along with all my accessories and waved me into the venue. I entered with only a spattering of light here and there to guide me. At first, I could only see the outlines of people—silhouettes against the shadowy background. As lights flickered and pulsated, I could see flashes of lace and skin. To my left, I caught a glimpse of glossy leather and metal accessories. Behind that, bright pink ropes were wrapped around a female figure who seemed almost oblivious to what was happening as she moved to the music. Before even turning on the camera I scanned the room and saw a mass of Afro-eroticism and liberation. A ball-gagged woman wearing nothing but a sheer catsuit grooved in the same space as the masked woman covered in a cloak that did nothing to cover the pasties and black thong underneath. The room had a sense of unbridled sexuality with an overarching playful and consensual tone. This was clearly going to be…unconventional.

This was not the first party I had shot and I never found them to be overly complicated. No matter how unique the host tried to make them it came down to the same basic elements. Browse the room, look for the most expressive people, and search for those personal moments between individuals that tell a story of the event. But house music changes things. It moves differently. There's no preoccupation with a preset list of favorite songs but rather an indescribable moment of sounds based on the feel of the crowd and energy in the room. It speaks with each dancer in the room and everyone responds whether they know it or not. That was my challenge, how do I find the personal moment in a room filled with personal moments.

I decided to start from one corner and work my way around the room, quietly navigating past the bodies in a personalized expression of inner sexuality. The loincloths around the masculine and feminine waists and black Gothic masks were accompanied by ankle-length cloaks and nude bodies, unless you count the body paint. My first stop was the corner of the venue that seemed to be designated for rope play. The bright pink rope that I had caught a glance of earlier was now spun around multiple women in various designs and configurations. It was easy to tell the difference between the curious and the experienced. Some looked on with a novice-like sense of wonder and others settled into relaxed states that made it apparent this was definitely not their first time. I moved deeper into the venue and walked directly into fishnet stockings wrapped around the legs of a tall woman. As I scanned up and passed the black lingerie, I stopped at the cat o' nine tails whip in her hand. Somehow, I didn't immediately see the willing participant bent over a chair, awaiting a moment of discipline. I was consumed with the figure and her commanding black whip. She playfully stalked her partner, staying with the beat of the music in the room. Light jabs became substantial hits that, with nonverbal consent, turned into heavy blows across the lower body. After one incredibly strong strike, the recipient stood and stared deeply at her whip-wielding aggressor. She took two steps forward and embraced her in an almost familial hug. Consent is beautiful.

I decided to follow the music and was struck by a tall, broad-shouldered figure towards the back of the venue. He stood behind a table filled with audio equipment, in full control of every sound coming out of the speakers. This was William Dunn, better known as DJ Big Will. To say Big Will makes an impression gives the word understatement new life. Living up to his moniker, he stands well past the six-foot mark with shoulders that seem the same length and a booming voice that seemed audible even when the music drowned out any other sound. He was the head DJ and was there at the beginning when Khari was still forming the event. House music always revolves around the DJs and each one speaks their own language with the tracks they select. Big Will's language was so pronounced and unique it was clearly the voice of Thee Debauchery Ball and everyone seemed to understand it intimately.

Suddenly, all attention was directed to the front of the venue. A band had almost covertly set up while people were distracted by the music and were now trying to gather people around with a series of announcements, guitar riffs, and drum rhythms. People started to migrate towards the seating area around the band, some with a sense of anticipation and some with high levels of curiosity. The band built to a mix of funk, soul, and gospel music. Suddenly a black-caped figure draped in silver Afrocentric jewelry took center stage. It was the man who had created everything I had experienced that night: Khari B.

I could describe Khari, I could find fancy words to explain to him as a person and an entertainer but I tend to avoid futility. I will simply say that if a tempest of art, charisma, and unfiltered commentary formed into a sentient being, Khari would still be more interesting. Commonly carrying the title of the "Disco Poet," he has been a paragon of the city's art scene for as long as I can remember. Matter of fact, if you want to out yourself as a tourist, simply state, "I don't know who Khari B is."

But this night he was a musician as much as a poet. Backed by the all-female band of his own creation dubbed "Osun's Waters," he took the stage bare-chested but nearly concealed in glimmering silver Afrocentric necklaces, medallions, and bracelets. He warmed up the crowd with a combination of introductions, instructions, and jokes. The first song was a surprising mix of rock and poetry with an erotic tone, which seemed to be a summation of the event itself. Each transition from song to song seemed to evoke another genre of music and each one had a unique poetic flow. I realized that this mix of genres was his non-verbal way of stating an overarching theme of the event and the culture around it. It's all house, it's all accepted, and it's all about community.

As the band began to wind down and peoples' attention turned back to the DJ, I was certain that I had captured enough footage for multiple projects, but I couldn't leave. I realized what I saw. I saw beauty, sexuality, no exploitation, no shame, judgments and inhibitions left at the door, and friends and lovers enjoying a safe space. There were stories upon stories but one thing seemed clear, this was never just about sex, it was never just about lust. This was a living art exhibit, an exhibition of community freedom and expression. We need more of this whether we realize it or not.

As the final song played and lights were slowly turned on, I gathered my equipment and headed toward the exit with almost the same crowd I entered with at the beginning of this journey. We rounded the same corner and rode down in the same elevator. As I opened the door and was hit with the same Chicago winter air I knew things were different. This needed to be documented, but its clandestineness needed to be protected. It needed to be celebrated and kept safe from those who would exploit it. But at that moment, in the frigid night air, one trivial thought would not leave my mind. I'm so glad I found parking.

Aug 14th, 2017—"Baptism"

ZUGGIE TATE

I found religion in a midnight DM
  Under a pseudonym
He said   call me Daddy
  And much akin to the Father
He built an alter on my lower back and knelt to pray

My toes curled
My eyes rolled to the back of my head And I
  swore I saw the face of God

What curse did you put on me?

Oracle to heavenly bodies,
  Slave to flesh
Eyes crossed into crucifix
I communicated in Moans
  Convulsed,
Sang the cry of devotion
Felt the cold throb of deception
  Felt the sting
Realized, you made me the sacrifice

To whom do I confess these midnights?
  Address these tears?
    Do I write this letter, stain each word with
      shame? Send it to my mother? My father?

In the presence of ancestors who came before me
I rubbed my skin with ash, wore sackcloth, begged forgiveness It's a
  sin a follow false idols
Yet everyone wants to be worshiped

...want an adoration that hurts a little
My grandmother warned of men like you
Men who come like thieves in the night

He'd appear like an apparition
  Fading in and out of time
I made my body his vessel To
  tether him to this moment A
  living sacrifice

Where did these chains come from? I
  didn't consent to bondage,
    ...To punishment
    ...To the gossip of prophetic storytellers
    ...To one-way conversations with piles of dead earth
    ...To the losing of my body, boundaries and self

My mother wept for her mistakes being born again in me The
  giving of my body to fickle ghost, holy spirits
    Who haunt doorways
      Who vanish in sunlight
      Who are powerful enough to move furniture
But are not powerful enough to stay

To whom do I confess these midnights?
  Address these prayers?
    To God? To this or that god? To
      the Devil?
    Each a hungry stomach waiting for an offering

[...]

I awake from the dream
  With blood on my hands
For it was I who had been killing myself all along Me,
  the willing sacrifice
But today, I'll find a new religion
    In loving myself, and licking my wounds

Burn

JANICE N. HARRINGTON

The wind then, through seams of bluestem,
or switchgrass swayed by a coyote's passing.

Where the fabric gapes, Barthes said,
lies the sensual. A prairie cut

by winding seeps, or winds or shearing wings.
Mare's tails, mackerels, cirrus,

distance dispersed as light. Under a buzzard's bank
and spiral the prairie folds and unfolds.

Here between the stands of bluestem, I am interruption.
I rake my fingers over culms and panicles.

Here seeds burr into my sleeves, spur each hem.
In a prairie, I am chance. I am rupture. The wind—

thief, ruffian, quick-fingered sky, snatches a kink
of my hair. The broken nap falls, wound round

like a prairie snake, a coil of barbed wire, a snare
for the unwary. In the fall, volunteer naturalists

will wrench invading roots and scour grassy densities
with fire. Wick, knot, gnarl, my kindled hair

will flare, burn, soften into ash, ash that will settle,
sieve through soil, compost for roots to suck

and worms to cast out, out into the loess that raises
redtop, turkeyfoot, sideoats grama,

and all the darkened progenies of grass
that reach and strive and shape dissent from light.

Originally published in Poem-A-Day, Academy of American Poets, on July 26, 2018.

Paintings
LESLIE BARLOW

Grandmother and Child
2019
Oil, pastel, acrylic, sewn fabric on panel, 48" x 48"

Ellen Barlow
2019
Oil, pastel, acrylic, photo transfer, sewn fabric on panel, 60" x 48"

Snowy Day
2019
Oil, pastel, acrylic, sewn fabric on panel, 48" x 48"

Joe's Ode

DEMAR WALKER

He hued crimson like Mississippi clay
A makeshift's tale etched into the Delta horizon
Dreamscapes of factories & Ford pristine
Wisconsin wayward to many akin
Rust stained alley ways kept his secrets
His jive I wish I spoke
Sworn oaths of big body sedans & local politicians
Rituals of flat tire repairs
Bike adventures to Lake Michigan
I am one of the boys, his boy
Their blues eclipsed by our jazz
"Did you get that lesson?!"
To be in good graces, I answered yes
Only to return with teams of confection
My penny candy to his moon pies
Slide to third base
Body slam off the ropes
No sport could match
For he was art
Personified
Dripped in the syrup of a blackberry tree
Driver's cap
Trouser slick
Couch comfy with crossed legs
Mason jar of Coca Cola on ice
Marlboro fancy
Rendezvous with the evening news
Peanut brittle & spare change
An elder's token
Love shared amongst both of us

... for, about, and with Laurie

BEVERLY COTTMAN

silence presses
    I listen with eyes wide open

sure enough it comes
a fluttering of hands preceding utterances just for me
   and for those who are here

and for those who are coming
and for those who have been

straining to hear
even more to comprehend

each word floats   then swirls
as if a halo
      encasing, infusing

silence presses
    I listen with eyes wide open

straining for what can only be heard on the wind

I know it is there
         she said it would be

water penetrating rock
     with the forcefulness of stars

murdered from my life
         leaving me behind
alone on my own path

     over the shoulder glances
     provide direction

inspired by where we have been

from "Call & Response: Experiments in Joy"

GABRIELLE CIVIL

"Without a discourse of their own, Black women artists remain fixed in the trajectory of displacement, hardly moving beyond the defensive posture of merely responding to their objectification and misrepresentation by others."
—Freida High W. Tesfagiorgis, "In Search of a Discourse and Critique/s that Center the Art of Black Women Artists"

Call & Response was born from an astral e-mail exchange with the then President of Antioch College, Mark Roosevelt, who was checking in with me about a job offer. At the time, I had been securely ensconced as an Associate Professor of English, Women's Studies and Critical Studies of Race & Ethnicity at a small, predominantly women's college in the Upper Midwest. I had worked there for thirteen years and had been tenured for six. I had not initially been seeking a new job, had not done a full search on the job market, but I had grown restless in the snowy heartland. I was seeking new ways to grow as an artist and teacher. I wanted—and still want—to become a better and better-known artist.

So when my friend Miré Regulus sent me the Performance job listing for Antioch out of the blue, my heart welled up. Here was an opportunity to align my extensive artistic practice and community teaching as a Black feminist performance artist with my professional identity. This position would be to build and lead an undergraduate Performance program with the notion of Performance as interdisciplinary and deliberately linked to Visual Arts and Media Arts. The position would allow me to test and develop my pedagogical ideas about experimental performance and consider key questions of performance art practice within a liberal arts context. More importantly, the job could shake me up, challenge me, and push me to put my money where my mouth is.

At the same time, accepting a job at Antioch would mean venturing into the cornfields, living in a tiny town (Yellow Springs, OH, pop. 3734) far from the dynamic art centers that had been my lifeblood (New York, Minneapolis, Mexico City). The thought excited and unnerved me. That spring of 2013, I had interviewed and received a job offer from Antioch, then asked for a week to decide whether or not to make the leap. During that time, Mark sent me a message, the exact words of which have been wiped away with the rest of the e-mail correspondence from my old life. It went something like:

"Dear Gabrielle,
I always think that March will be warm, but today again is cold and rainy. But then I thought, maybe something good will happen today. Maybe Gabrielle will write me about coming to Antioch."

To that, I responded something like:

"Dear Mark,
I have been dreaming about the cornfields . . . My biggest fear of coming to Antioch College is losing my context, the people, places, things, situations that allow me and my work to make sense. One thing that would help allay that fear would be a festival of Black women and performance at Antioch College, an opportunity to bring Black women performers together from around the country, presenting and sharing work with each other and Antioch students. This would be magical."

Although the possibility of a Black women's performance festival had long been percolating in my mind—indeed Rosamond S. King, Wura-Natasha Ogunji and I had tossed it around separately at various times—I had no idea that I would propose this idea until I did. The flash of insight to write this to Mark that day can only be described as a gift from God, although others could as easily thank the universe, killer instinct, or #blackgirlmagic.

To my surprise and delight, Mark immediately responded: "This is the best e-mail I think I have ever received. Let me ask around and see if we can actually make this happen…" Mark's instant enthusiasm helped convince me to give Antioch a try. Because I proposed this idea at a key moment and the institution agreed to support it, the Call & Response symposium of Black Women & Performance took place at Antioch College. May more such miracles come to pass.

Call & Response Artist Show & Tell (July 2014)

The seven lead artists of Call & Response were (from left to right) Awilda Rodríguez Lora from San Juan, Puerto Rico; Rosamond S. King from Brooklyn, NY; Wura-Natasha Ogunji then based in both Austin, Texas and Lagos, Nigeria, now fully relocated to Lagos; Miré Regulus from Minneapolis; Kenyatta A. C. Hinkle from Los Angeles; myself Gabrielle Civil, project organizer, newly relocated to Yellow Springs, OH; and, Duriel E. Harris from Chicago. Our practice represented a full gamut of performance from multi-media performance art, live art actions, performance installation, theater, dance, music, conceptual art, spoken word, poetry, and more. Moreover, each artist had significant experience with more than one performance form. We also had various diasporic connections to Africa and the Caribbean and represented a range of ages, academic backgrounds, sexual orientations, familial situations, gender experiences, languages spoken, and more. Even more significantly, none of the artists, myself included, had met all of the other ones. While many of us ran in the same circles or had heard each other's names, the symposium became an opportunity to build community as Black women performers and make new artistic connections.

_____ is the thing with feathers-Gabrielle Civil
premiered at the Experiments in Joy Performance Festival
Call & Response: Black Women & Performance at Antioch College

Installation
A red and yellow plastic rug.
A yellow suitcase full of paper upstage
with a red roll of masking tape stuck through the handle.
A yellow and red rubber chicken downstage.
A video projection looming large above:
a black and white drawing
of a black woman with scars.

Overture
"Ode to Joy" from Beethoven's Symphony No. 9 in D Minor, Op 125
starts to play and continues to play throughout the next sequence.

Vèvè Chicken Threshold
I walk through the aisles with the rubber chicken,
stirring it into space—stirring up voodoo ritual and new world culture
The crowd starts to apprehend "the thing without feathers" ...

Chicken Fusion
I pull out the roll of red tape and let the expanse spread between my hands.
I tape the rubber chicken to my body
and let it circle and circle around my body.
Red tape holds the rubber chicken in place around my waist.

Red Tape Scars
Once the rubber chicken is secure, I make red tape scars.
I tear off small pieces of red tape and press them all over my body.
Beethoven starts to fade.

Into Blackness
The slide changes.
A video projection appears with the title of this work:
"_____ is the thing with feathers"
I say: "And what does it mean to be without feathers?"

I wait two beats and then the slide changes again to black.
The backdrop remains black for the rest of the show.

<u>Into the Paper</u>
I say: "So when I came to Yellow Springs,
I brought approximately a million boxes
and bags and suitcases of paper."
I open up the yellow suitcase, set and spread out stacks of paper.

"Years ago, when I was trying to become myself,
I would gather all this, black women's poems, plays, essays,
and I would hoard it and cherish it and keep it close.

This was before the internet.
And when someone gave you a copy
of an article about black women's dreaming,
you held onto it for dear life.
You carried it with you wherever you went
because you weren't sure if you lost it,
you would ever be able to find these words again.

I move the papers through my hands.
I make designs of the stacks of paper on the stage.
The paper is black women's paper, black women's dreaming.

"What is the urgency of our invention?
How can we undefine the defined?

What is irresistible to us?
And what if we can let go, transform the past
and turn it into something new?"

Feathers

I reach into the yellow suitcase and find a pair of red-handled scissors.
I cut a feather from black women's paper.
I tape that feather to my body.

There are more scissors in the suitcase.
I walk out into the crowd and hand scissors to people.
I invite them to come and make feathers from the stacks of paper.
to tape those feathers onto my body, onto themselves and each other.

is the thing with feathers
And when it seems like we are almost ready for flight,
I say: "_____ is the thing with feathers.
And what is the _____?"
Hope! a poetry reader calls.
"Ah someone knows their Emily D!
Okay, but here and now we're in the experiment
so what else can _____ be?"

The crowd calls out new possibilities.
Memory! Love! Letting go!

I encourage the cacophony of sound,
And as the space fills with words,
like feathers rustling in space.
I return to the suitcase and roll out a long runway
made of this black woman's paper.
Longer than my arms, I find two long wings
made of black women's paper.

Joy!
Bettye Levette's song "Joy" fades in.
It starts soft and gets louder and louder.

I say: "This is the runway. This is the landing strip.
I have my feathers. Now these are my wings."

I take my place at the end of the runway.
I prepare my arms with undulation.
I prepare my legs with dance.

My red tape scars and my yellow and red rubber chicken
are still there but are now engulfed by this paper.

I run. I jump. I use my wings made of words.
I shout out the word "Joy!" each time I rise in air.
I fly.

Performance photos by Dennie Eagleson

First published in Obsidian: Literature & Arts in the African Diaspora, *volume 41.1-2, Fall 2015. It also appears in the performance memoir* Experiments in Joy *by Gabrielle Civil, published in 2019 by Civil Coping Mechanisms/the Accomplices.*

IV.
NOW

But that's the problem with knowing. It takes away the possibility of pretending.
—Pearl Cleage

(Raised in Detroit, Michigan)

Photographs

RACHEL ELISE THOMAS

Since 1983, Freedom House Detroit has accepted thousands of refugees and families who are seeking asylum from the countries they're fleeing. This body of work chronicles the individuals seeking asylum and the unique circumstances which led them to Detroit. With this series, I am demonstrating that a meaningful story can be told without revealing the subject's identity. In addition to photography, the residents' handwriting, thoughts, opinions, drawings, etc. is incorporated. This gives my subjects personality and voice because often the media depicts asylum seekers as two-dimensional and not as actual people.

Vision: This particular Freedom House resident is proud of the clean room that he once shared with a roommate. He explained to me that he won't have the room to himself for long once another male that's in the same predicament moves into the house. This and other things were discussed in Detroit, MI on Tuesday, November 6, 2018.

Positive Vibes: This Freedom House resident is proud of her hair. Her locs are a symbol of her resilience and inner and outer beauty. This and other meaningful things were discussed in Detroit, MI on Thursday, November 14, 2018.

Afternoon Games: Freedom House Detroit is located in Southwest Detroit, an area of the city that is known for its Mexican community, culture, and neighborhoods. Here, adolescent boys play basketball in the parking lot of Saint Anne Catholic Parish that is located next to the organization in Detroit, MI on November 28, 2018.

I Just *want* to say that
I didn't want to come in
USA in these case of
situation but I didn't
have any choice and I
Just want to say that
Sometimes we can not
know what is gonna
happen Tomorrow.
,and I use To say I
came here For study
I don't have To answer
a lot of questions.
every asylum siour had
a story which make
him or her fled his
or her country.

Every Asylum Seeker Had a Story: I asked a group of Freedom House residents: "Based on your circumstance and people's misconceptions about someone seeking asylum, what do you want people to know about you?" In their own words and writing, an authentic and honest response was given. This and other meaningful things were discussed on Friday, January 4, 2019.

A Minute, A Pond, A North-Facing Window

KIM-MARIE WALKER

A speck of peppa in a sea of salt,
This black body exists in white suburbia
Green-spaces with cleaner air, bike paths, and eagle flyovers
This black body craves existence
marked by miles of open sky, lakes, wildlife, and trees
Not blue eyes, or slow roving police cars marking
This black body walking round the block, cycling round lakes
like Becky does without hesitation
A speck of salt in a sea of salt

The pond surface is half open water, half frozen over with a thin ice layer, no snow. Both stilled surfaces reflect a row of shoreline pine trees—olive green boughs with dark gray and brown trunks. Eyes on the pond, I watch stringy gray clouds inch eastward under pale blue sky.

Suddenly, the pond's mirror image captures two ravens flying overhead, flanking a hawk. I glance up, to track hawk's cruise through raven territory, and down to movement on the pond. A muskrat has emerged from an edge of ice. Its silky glide ripples water toward muddy tunnels submerged on the northwest bank.

Then, incredibly, hundreds of geese in staggered V-formations fly overhead, just fifty feet above nearby cottonwood trees. A quick slide of the window lets me hear a hoarse concerto of honks and wings whooshing. For seconds, the pond mirrors feathered creatures journeying south.

Clouds pick up speed from the west. A breeze dapples the pond surface, mixes with the undulating V-wake inspired by the muskrat crossing. Sixty seconds have passed.

My heart struggles to make room for gratitude and to dropkick mid-morning's gloom. I've internalized law enforcers latest killing of an unarmed Black man and assault of an unarmed teenage Black girl, of a Black baby shot in urban crossfire. These recent events, as gut-wrenching add-ons to decades of observing how systemic institutional racism plays out on so many levels, may tip me into depression's abyss.

And though no blue-clad officer has ever touched me, my body knows invasion. I've banged my mind against a wall and there are fractures. Every millimeter crack, an instance of trying to filter human suffering. Every exuberance at being alive competes with internal screaming. Astonishing how screams erupt without sound.

From the pond's viewpoint all that has passed overhead and through is eternal. Everlasting in the molecules and nanoparticles of elements draining into the creek into the lake and into that, which overtime, evaporates to the cyclical interplay of air, water, and plant photosynthesis. All of which I'm dependent upon. Am one with.

Oneness with all things is not a choice. It is the state of existence.

Living with this paradox is hard. Me, the humanitarian *and* the terrorist. Citizen *and* police. Disrupter *and* critic. Consumer *and* polluter.

Living with this paradox is easy. Me, the pond *and* the raven. Blue sky mid-morning *and* inky star-filled night. Pond ripples *and* a singular wave crashing ashore.

When thoughts and words fail to marvel, this mid-morning observation tilts numbness and gloom toward resilience, toward zealous activism to hold accountable each internal fracture, those long, exasperating exhales, those silent screams.

For the rest of the day, my struggle for gratitude dissolves. Sixty seconds of pond's reveal, remembered, relived.

I am a landlocked body

ALEXANDRA NICOME

Reckless, I dance among these cluttered annals of unclaimed thoughts and discarded ideas. Why bother with ingenuity when I can scavenge for something unfinished, unremembered, or unsaid? Why bother finishing, remembering, or saying? I'd rather shuffle through this rootless soil of things unknown; dig wet ground in pursuit of clarity; sow seeds in this fruitless slip all the while wondering: if mud is always dirty, will this work ever be clean?

Hapless and listening, I learn that I've inherited everything primal and nothing original. They forged a lineage of beasts, savages, and deviants. Bloodless and endlessly replicant. Alarmed, the climate concerned, demographically conscious, and racially anxious dominants say "dystopia." They power over but fail to eclipse the other: stupid, lazy, shifty, dangerous, unknowable,
mysterious amorphous

nebulous

dark
under
downwards
creaks
'neath
nadir

Right beneath you, this is the middle. Defiantly ambiguous and *anticoherent*. Here, coherence as a rule operates in service of domination and control. Descending through bureaucracy towards me, bending in my direction, upon me, in spite of itself, bearing the likes of me, coherence feels my fullness and capsizes
it witnesses
a baffling vastness
animated

lucid contours careening crumbling
croak
ing swish ing
swish splat
gurgle gape gasp grasp grin
rasp reek realizing
shallow waters
scrutiny surfaces
ears pop
evidencing pressure
emerges an imposter.

A PRAYER.

Oh dear mask please again and forever let it be damned,
your domesticated seed, your dusking veil, your landlocked destiny,
again and forever damn you because

Columbus: Different Latitude, Same Platitudes

DEVA RASHED-BOONE

Columbus, Ohio became my newest home in the fall of 2015, and conversations with so many of my loved ones from my last home, St. Louis, Missouri, commenced with the earnest inquiry, "How is Columbus?"

Ever the hopeful realist and not having yet experienced any wholly negative interactions in my new home, I'd simply reply "Columbus is... different." After all, if Columbus was anything at all to me at that time, it was...different. The PTSD-inducing, palpable, racist segregation and profuse gun violence I encountered all too often in my beloved St. Louis were now 400 miles west of me, bridged only by the persistence of my memories and I-70. Every attempt at describing the nature of what this "difference" entailed, in some way or another, involved a depiction of the mystifying civility of the white people with whom I'd interacted.

Just one year earlier, in 2014, I'd lived through the traumatic events of Ferguson—the fatality and the fallout. The barbarous slaughter of Mike Brown Jr. and the subsequent attempts to suppress the righteous indignation that ensued were impossible to ignore as a resident of St. Louis City and an employee of the City of Berkeley, a municipality bordering Ferguson. Far too few people understood then that the eruption in Ferguson was not about allegedly stolen convenience store merchandise or perceived non-compliance with law enforcement agents. There are Fergusons waiting to happen everywhere the presence of Black, Brown and poor bodies becomes an inconvenience to the supposed "progress" of those who benefit from the original theft of land from Indigenous peoples. To be clear, the entirety of what is recognized as the United States of America is stolen land, and the presence of Black, Brown, and poor people will always be an "inconvenience" that threatens progress.

In the early days of my time in Columbus, I roomed with a dear friend from college in the neighborhood of Olde Towne East. Our home, his house, was directly across from Kwanzaa Park, doors down from historic mansions, three minutes away from my job, and in the eye of a raging storm of gentrification. The eyes of storms are always so peaceful, but ever-shifting and prone to leave behind spaces that fail to remain peaceful.

Just a little more than a year later, two years after the killing of Mike Brown, Jr., the shifting of the eye of Columbus's gentrification storm would result in law enforcement ending the young life of Tyre King in cruelly extrajudicial fashion in the Olde Towne East neighborhood. Tyre was the same age of the students, "My Babies," whom I had moved to Columbus to serve in my new role as a middle school administrator, and while I did not know him personally, a number of my friends had the joy and pleasure of having played a role in his life. While the violent manner in which his life was snatched away hit close to home, my already traumatized psyche wouldn't permit me to process at the time exactly how similar his death was to the one that occurred in Ferguson just two years earlier. I'd not forgotten Michael Brown—both what his life said about him and what his killing said about a nation that has been perpetually at odds with the presence of Black bodies in any capacity other than as chattel slaves. It was this connection, more than any other, that made Columbus eerily similar to St. Louis, St. Louis to Detroit, Detroit to Atlanta, and Atlanta to Washington, D.C.

A native of rural Southeast Texas, each of my relocations to a new city, first to St. Louis then to Columbus, initially represented an opportunity to inch ever northward, above the Mason-Dixon line and long-held racist beliefs. However, Columbus demonstrated in 2016, as St. Louis had in 2014, that there is no latitude or elevation at which the potentially deadly dangers of racism and white supremacy can be escaped, unless its propagators elevate their understanding of what constitutes true humanity. To do this, they must gain the understanding that the systematic dehumanization of others, whereby gentrification becomes the means and end to remove inconvenient Black, Brown, and poor bodies, erodes the humanity of all involved.

The Reality of Being Black in Iowa

WYLLIAM SMITH

When I was about to graduate from high school in Grand Rapids, Michigan, many people ridiculed me for only applying to three colleges. My classmates had applied to eight or nine colleges and insisted that I needed to broaden my options. But I didn't need to apply to fifteen schools because I knew that no matter what happened, I was going to the University of Iowa.

I wanted to go to UI because I'm a writer, and this university is ranked No. 1 in the nation for its writing program. When I told my family my decision, my mother said, "Enjoy all the white people and the corn."

She was joking of course. Regardless I ignored everyone's warnings and came here anyway. I didn't think about my race, money, or location when I moved here. In my mind, none of that mattered. I had secured a job at the UI newspaper *The Daily Iowan*, I was getting a degree for a career I loved, I was making connections with great writers, and I was following my dreams. It never occurred to me that being one of 1,035 Black students in a school of 33,564 students would be a problem.

It's been two years since I first visited UI to sign my registration papers. Now, I see the uglier side of Iowa. I see the kids crossing to the other side of the street when I walk by. I notice professors complimenting me on how "articulate" I am. I hear conversations cease when I walk into the room.

"Sometimes the shitty part is you don't know if it's in your head or if it's actually happening," said UI senior Sam Osaro, who is involved in Hubbard Scholars, a black male support group on campus, as well as the National Association of Black Journalists.

I felt crazy. People told me I was being overly dramatic, or that I was looking for racism in society, and that's why I kept seeing it. It was always my fault people were being racist, or the problems were all in my head and I was fabricating racism where there is none.

"As somebody who studies race, I can say that things aren't just in people's heads," said Jessica Welburn, a UI assistant professor of sociology and African American Studies. "I've gone into the CVS in the mall and felt like I was being watched and followed … And I knew that [the CVS employee] would never guess that I was a faculty member on campus."

After my first year at the UI, I started to embrace my Blackness and there was a massive backlash. Whenever I tried to speak out against racist practices, both in my classes and when I wrote for the *DI*, I was met with hate mail and bigotry.

When I grew my hair out, I was told it was nappy. When I wore a hoodie to my job, someone said I looked "ghetto." After I wrote the story "Why the University of Iowa Needs Black-Only Events," I received an email from "mlucky99" that said, "Can we get our drinking fountains back too. It goes both ways young man. Be careful what you wish for …"

The UI campus claims it's diverse, and its motto is, "You Are Welcome Here," but everywhere I turn I feel as if I am being told, "I am not welcome." Some UI students feel the campus is "anti-Black."

Black student activist and UI senior Matthew Bruce has described his experience of being Black at the University as being as difficult. He said that people told him his natural hair, dreadlocks, are unprofessional with some suggesting he change it for job interviews.

"The only way for Black students to be engaged in the University is to dethrone their identity of being Black and to become white," said UI senior Latrell Burden. Burden said that Black students are forced to conform to white culture to be seen as legitimate and relevant, and any move to embrace Black culture is seen as disreputable.

"My initial gut reaction is no, [UI is] not anti-Black." said Nadine Petty, the executive director of the Center for Diversity and Enrichment in response. "I think what the campus is, is status quo, and the status quo here on this campus is white. Most of the campus community who are decision-makers are white; which means most of the programming, and the services, and the campus-focused activities are going to come from a lens that is also white. And that's not necessarily anti-Black, but it's not pro-Black either."

Personally, I find that people at the UI liked me more when I was being complicit in the racist beliefs on campus. They liked it when I forced myself to laugh at stereotypes, such as "all Black men are criminals." They did not like it when I wrote stories dissecting those racist beliefs, such as my DI article "Acting Black, Acting the Part."

Although, when I come forward and say that this campus is not a place where Black students thrive, I am met with the same five-worded response: "You chose to come here."

Some would argue because of that fact alone, Black students should get over it. We did, after all, choose to go to this school. Yes, I chose to go here, but I chose to come here because I love to write. I chose to come here to meet and learn from writers from all over the world. I did not come here to suffer racism both in and out of the classroom. I didn't choose to be insulted and belittled by a campus that values whiteness over inclusivity.

The idea that Black individuals should "know what they are getting into" is asinine to me. I am not expecting the University of Iowa population to have a percentage of Black students that is in the double digits, but that does not excuse both subtle, and blatant, racism that Black students must face every day. Saying that racism is just a product of being Black in the Midwest is the reason it still exists.

A version of this essay first appeared in The Daily Iowan *on May 1, 2018.*

Ode to unwanted life

ZENZELE ISOKE

Sixty-two unopened
envelopes from my non-profit
credit union did not push me out
of my updated early twentieth century
Henry Longfellow bungalow.

Star-shaped petals of
wild phlox thriving
in the coffee hull mulch
beside
baby heirlooms
made voluntary black
dispossession
a smart economic
choice.

Flourishing of clover
alongside dried up
stalks of tiger lilies and
anemic bunches
of corporate sage
forced me
into surrender.

Not eight credit cards
pushing sky-high limits
with monthly late fees and
compounding interest
or even the
criminal antics of a
billionaire gigolo
named Wells Fargo
who served me
mercilessly for
ten years.

It was morning glory
happy and sturdy
nestled between
superabundant rows
of flowering collards
cucumber corn
and giant zucchini.

No, no, no not cracks
        in the foundation
        in the paint
        or cracks
in the salmon
hexagon mini-tiles
into which
tiny waves of
greasy black mold
would sometimes seep.

Not accumulating
deferred interest
on undergraduate aid
offered twenty years prior.

Blue thistle priced me out
of my gentrifying neighborhood
in South Minneapolis
where I raised two lucky
black female souls
who outperformed
birth controls pills
condoms
rhythm methods
and a hard-won inclination
to use
my dwindling right to
abortion.

Wild bursts of
yellow dock
primrose
rosettes of shepherd's purse

and my very first childhood friend
lion's tooth
whose golden yellow discs
I gathered up
and watched wilt in my small hands
even before
I could cross
the abandoned
glass-strewn street
and climb the stairs
of a brick faced house
where
a used plastic
cup of tap water
sat on the
kitchen table
of a North Saint Louis
single family home
my grandmama
owned for more than fifty years
before she died.

The unwantedness
of flowers
otherwise called weeds
I had not the
time or money
or will to
kill
revealed
the murderous
futility of ownership
in an American dream
built
on the disappearance
of unwanted life.

Trying to Make a Dollar Out of Fifteen Cents in Black Milwaukee

GLADYS MITCHELL-WALTHOUR

This essay argues that Black women Supplemental Nutrition Assistance Program (SNAP) beneficiaries resist the manifestations of white supremacy in the necropolitical city of Milwaukee. Through the narratives of these women it is clear they practice multiple strategies such as relying on family members, bargaining with apartment owners, and seeking work when facing economic hardships. Interviews are part of a larger project that compares the political opinions of African descended women in Brazil and the USA. While most of my research focuses on Brazil, after moving to Milwaukee, as a Black woman, mother of a black child, and wife to a Black man, the necropolitical nature of the city felt familiar as I have conducted research in Brazil. Necropolitics describes life as death due to racism, colonialism, and slavery (Mbembe 2019). Jaime Alves notes that necropolitics involve the actions of state agents, namely the police who view blacks as nonbeings. Alves says that in the anti-Black city of São Paulo, death while living is a part of the black experience as blacks in low income neighborhoods are policed and executed and slum communities (favelas) are prison-like spaces while actual prisons are favelas in their structures. Much like this Brazilian city, in Milwaukee, a city that is 40 percent Black, Blacks are in a state of social death.

The Black infant mortality rate in Milwaukee is 18.1 compared to 3.6 for whites (Dennis 2019). While living in Milwaukee, I suffered two miscarriages. Like other Black mothers, the necropolitics of the city leaves Black women in a state of living death and part of life is death, in that future Black children are dead before being born. While most Blacks in Milwaukee live on the Northside, I live in a suburb of the university which is only 2.3% Black. I also have educational degrees from elite universities and am a professor. Yet the institutionalization of racism in public places such as restaurants, coffee shops, and hospitals does not make me immune from stereotypes people have about Black women. Thus, although my social class is quite different from low-income Black women in Milwaukee, I am stereotyped in much the same way as low-income Black women.

Milwaukee is consistently ranked as the worst place for African Americans and Black children to live. Children who are born and live in the inner city in low-income neighborhoods suffer in under-resourced and poor performing schools where black students are more likely to receive harsher disciplinary action than non-Blacks. It has high incarceration rates and the highest level of residential segregation of any other metropolitan city in the USA. The Black poverty rate in Milwaukee is 30.3 compared to 10 for whites (Smeeding and Thornton 2018). The Black unemployment rate is twice that of whites. African American households' median incomes in Milwaukee are $28,928 a year compared to $66,097 for white households (Watson 2019). Like many Brazilian cities, Milwaukee is anti-Black.

I make the Black feminist claim that surviving in a necropolis and anti-Black city is a form of politics and resistance. Discrimination, colorism, sexism, and segregation make employment difficult. Food assistance makes it possible for women to feed their families in the necropolis of Milwaukee. Black women fight for daily survival. In 2017, research assistant, Elijah Nicks and myself interviewed 20* Black women SNAP beneficiaries. Demographic data on employment status, skin tone, and age were collected given that Black women with darker skin colors have lower levels of marriage rates, regardless of educational attainment (Hamilton, Goldsmith, and Darity 2009). This essay focuses on how they survive when facing financial constraints. In his research, Alves asks "How does one navigate a social world in which life is lived through a cumulative process of dying (day-to-day humiliation, deprivation, criminalization, and finally physical death... (69)." While I do not focus on police brutality, my research is similar in that death is not simply physical death but dying which entails deprivation of food, employment opportunities, the loss of life before life, exclusion from civil life and everyday humiliations. Like the adage, "how do low income Black women make a dollar out of fifteen cents?" I analyze responses to the interview question, "Has it ever been difficult to pay bills and make ends meet and if so, what do you do in those circumstances?" Most women rely on family members when they are short on cash. Others rely on budgeting, frugality, and payment arrangements with landlords. A few rely on God as a source of survival and some believe readily acquiring a job is an option.

---

*The author thanks Elijah Nicks for assisting with interviews and all participants who dedicated their time to participate.

Family as a Source of Survival

Matthew Desmond's book *Evicted: Power and Profit in the American City* details the struggles of low-income people who are evicted in Milwaukee, which has some of the highest eviction rates in the country. When rent is paid, families may become short on other bills. SNAP benefits assist families with food purchases, but in many cases families have other household bills. Twenty-eight percent of women in this sample said they relied on family members when it was difficult to pay bills. A 35-year-old dark-skinned unemployed single woman responded: "Um yeah it's always difficult, so you network with people around you experiencing the same thing... Ya'll money may come around different times of the month [so you] just network with friends and family and ask." Further she states, "Yeah borrow or just network... We gone eat over here... What you cookin'? [We] kind of compromise." In this case, she reveals that she may borrow from friends but also a system of exchange may occur where a friend may provide food for a friend and they can rely on that same person to provide for her family when they are in a bind.

A 42-year-old dark-skinned single woman and former SNAP beneficiary who currently works as a registered nurse stated:

> There's times where I've been in subsidized housing that has helped... but when I was not in subsidized housing, there were things that I went without. I always tried to keep my phone on but um there was no entertainment and... food was always low um I used the food pantry before... [I] borrowed money very seldom. I'm not that type of person but I had to borrow money to eat... I've just had to cut a lot of corners... I've had... electricity cut off about two times in my life... but I've gotten really good at budgeting things... so that hasn't happened in a while.

The highest number of respondents answered they rely on friends and family during rough times. Social ties to family and friends aid in survival.

Delayed Gratification and Frugality

Unlike Ronald Reagan's welfare queen trope, a stereotype of black women who receive government assistance and spends money on extravagant items, 17 percent of these participants engage in delayed gratification and frugality as a means of survival when in economic straits. This is best demonstrated in a 26-year-old AmeriCorps member who lives with her parents. She contributes to the household by paying the electric bill and she budgets her money. She practices delayed gratification and budgeting. She stated, "I can't buy that new purse that I want. I can't buy those new pair of shoes that I want… I'm learning to budget."

Another example of frugality is a 42-year-old single woman with a medium complexion who is unemployed and disabled. She shopped when there were sales and asked family members for money when in financial hardship. For those who availed employment status, 67 percent were unemployed. As noted earlier, Black unemployment in Milwaukee is significantly higher than white unemployment which, I argue, is due to discrimination; a characteristic of the necropolis. Yet these thrifty women highlight the ways in which they spend wisely and delay instant gratification as a means of survival, thus defying the pervasive controlling image (Collins 1990) of Black women as lazy welfare queens.

Arrangement with Landlord

Eleven percent of the sample made rent payment arrangements with the landlord. Desmond (2016) finds that often these arrangements become burdensome to landlords and the consequences are detrimental to families who can be evicted. In this sample, women did not report eviction as landlords were willing to work with them. However, at least one participant was living in a shelter with her 3-month-old baby. The following are responses of two participants who discuss making payment arrangements;

A dark-skinned 34-year-old mother of two who was unemployed stated, "I've gone to different agencies and acquired temp[orary job] positions. I've gone to family members and I've gotten loans… [I've made] budget plans with WE energies you know, talking to my landlord, setting up [a payment plan] even if I gotta pay my rent in a split payment within the same month."

This respondent received loans, set up a payment plan with an energy company, and made arrangement to pay her rent. Taking these steps require time, especially for someone with two children. Yet such measures are taken for the survival of her family. Another participant does not have children and is a member of AmeriCorps, which pays a small stipend. She is a dark-skinned 23-year-old Jamaican-American woman who relies on her sister for small amounts of money. She discusses the difficulty of paying rent but says her landlady was willing to make arrangement with her since she's an AmeriCorps member. She states "I still don't know how… I pull through every month. But there was a time when I couldn't pay my rent and I was just freaking out a bit... cuz you know I live on my own." This participant was in a privileged position since her landlady was aware of the AmeriCorps program and was sympathetic.

Finding Work

Thirty-three percent of participants were employed. As mentioned earlier, the unemployment rate of Blacks is four times higher than the unemployment rate for whites. The necropolitical nature of the city, anti-blackness, and sexism lead to higher rates of Black unemployment compared to white unemployment. In addition, many of these interviews took place at the YWCA where women were seeking help, thus the participant sample is even more vulnerable than SNAP beneficiaries in general. Four participants, or 20 percent, said when faced with financial hardship, they look for employment. A 33-year-old employed single mother of three who has a college degree said when it is difficult to make ends meet, she finds another job that makes more money to cover her bills. A 35-year-old single mother of two and a college graduate who belongs to the prestigious sorority of Alpha Kappa Alpha Incorporated, has a medium skin tone, and is unemployed, said she starts working when it is difficult to pay bills. Another medium-complexioned woman who is 24-years-old and has one child, also answered she finds work. It is possible these women find work because they have completed high school and at least half completed college. However, the fact they need assistance shows the economic vulnerability of Black women, even those with higher education.

> Ohh I done borrowed. I done begged you know. I done robbed Peter to pay Paul. I mean ...only thing I haven't done is prostitute myself but I have you know, put myself in debt; you know what I'm sayin' just to make sure that my family is okay (Dark-skinned unemployed single mother of five children).

> I learned that Milwaukee is a women's city like they love to help women (26-year-old medium- complexioned woman with three children).

Conclusion

While the first above-mentioned quote acknowledges the difficulty of feeding one's family, the second quote from another participant is optimistic. This participant believes Milwaukee loves to help women. This woman's optimism is much like the women who believe obtaining work during economic difficulties is a possibility. This optimism is also a form of survival and resistance. These narratives of Black women SNAP beneficiaries show how they survive in a necropolitical city. Many rely on family and friend networks, some bargain to schedule rent payments, and others exhaust all measures to provide for their families. Colorism plays a role in disadvantage as 70 percent of participants are dark-skinned. As in Brazil, poverty has a color which is dark. Despite colorism, racism, and sexism, these women demonstrate agency. Black women in São Paulo create black spaces or a blackpolis (Alves 2018). Black women in Milwaukee create spaces of resistance in their homes and communities by surviving in a city where death and dying is a part of the lived black experience.

References

Alves, Jaime. 2018. *The Anti-Black City: Police Terror and Black Urban Life in Brazil*. Minneapolis: University of Minnesota Press.

Collins, Patricia Hill. 1990. *Black Feminist Thought: Knowledge, Consciousness, and the Politics of Empowerment*. Taylor and Francis.

Dennis, LaToya. "Milwaukee's Mortality Rate For Black Babies Is High. Why, And What's Being Done About It?" May 21, 2019.

Desmond, Matthew. 2016. *Evicted: Poverty and Profit in the American City*. Crown Publishers.

Hamilton, Darrick, Arthur Goldsmith, and William Darity. 2009. "Shedding "light" on marriage: The influence of skin shade on marriage for Black females" *Journal of Economic Behavior & Organization*. 72 (1): 30-50.

Mbembe, Achille. 2019. *Necropolitics*. Durham: Duke University Press.

Smeeding, Timothy and Katherine Thornton. September 2018. "Poverty, Incomes, Race and Ethnicity in Wisconsin and Milwaukee: A Supplement to the 2016 Poverty Report." https://www.irp. wisc.edu/wp/wp-content/uploads/2018/09/Supplement-WIPovRept-September2018.pdf

Watson, Alana. 2019. "Report: Milwaukee, Racine Rank As Worst Cities For African Americans To Live Milwaukee Ranks No. 1, Racine Ranks No. 2 For Worst City For African Americans." Wisconsin Public Radio. November 15, 2019.

It's Just OK

NIA EASLEY

It's Just Ok by Nia Easley was made possible by a grant from the Illinois Arts Council Agency, the Alphawood Foundation, and by Helis Foundation with support from Catherine Edelman through Threewalls.

t's just ok.

Ghetto Bird Wars

CURTIS L. CRISLER

(1) The city seagulls linger the Lowe's,
linger the Home Depot. For what? Seagulls
used to show cleverness, swoop out of Hitchcock's
head, or sweep the gritty sands of Lake Michigan,
kicking it la vida loca—dancing to hot hip-hop
and R&B. They had crazy West Side Story-
taloned-squabbles with gangster pigeons over
pieces of discarded day-old hot dog and cheese-
burger buns, or fake-dived, approaching a floating
dead fish killed by the mill's phosphorous, lining
shores from the Dunes to Chi-town. These Lowe's
seagulls roam off-kilter, a maddened translucence
of bulliness in emerald irises, like pattern mapped
in clever brains of a kin carrier pigeon (Original
Gangsters of all P.I.G.E.O.Ns). What brings
their white feathered rage to Fort Worths, Austins,
Ann Arbors, or Carbondales? Nature's natural
in strip-malls, lush in parking lot of Menards.
In shopping bliss, eyes up, we step in their feces.

                               (2) What motivates
white nomads to come from elsewhere is that
they have exploded caustic bombs on the heads
and laps and tits of those with pull—Thinkers.
Like all nomads, 'gulls think survival—Rambo,
and relocate because the Thinkers have put out hits,
and the Lingerers have become marks. Marks crave
for touch, for another to convince another of their
brotherhood within a city's limit. Blackberry crows
caw out dark literature from an opposing telephone
line, let the seagulls know how funny harboring
a place full of wood and fixtures and countertops
shows lapse in synapses, but seagulls wear resilience.

What's been documented, researched, is legend in
the Audubon's rustic back yard—amid Buddhist
monks. Cities fly-swat at venturing gangs ravaging
populace—seagulls who move in a full-throttle—
motoring bikers on roam soaring about, revving at
the Thinkers who feel the weekend is a freedom.
The Nomads-For-Life leave a Lowe's sky-looker
b i t c h i n g in red, white, or blue s p l a t t e r s.

On Audre Lorde and Minnesota Nice

VANESSA TAYLOR

"The sun goes down, the batons come up."

I went to Ferguson, Missouri in a van full of strangers. All of us went as a result of mobilization around Ferguson October but, beyond that, we were all brought by a break. Something—not the same thing for everybody, but something nonetheless—snapped inside all of us when Ferguson's uprising first began.

For me, it was a broken string located deep inside of my chest, somewhere to the left and behind my heart, so every one of its beats had an awkward, hollow twang. In the car ride down, I stared out the window and reflected on how strange it was to be surrounded by people I don't know. I'm not a people person, but I would find myself among strangers on the parking lot of the Ferguson Police Department, outside a Quick Trip, inside of two jail cells.

I made the comment about batons that opens this essay while sitting inside of a Hardee's as police officers stood at the ordering counter. Or maybe I said it while standing on a street whose name I can no longer recall, listening to the low drone of helicopters flying low overhead, metal bellies all that I could see. Maybe I said it while watching the sun set on itself, an awkward observer bowing out of the moment. Maybe I timed each word to the beat of the police's batons on the sidewalk as their line approached and I gripped the arms of the people around me tighter.

Wherever and however I said it, it was a joke. Being Black and young means coming from a tradition of making a comedy sketch out of your own suffering. It is meant for select consumption, the type of "oh, that's so *wrong*" laughter that eventually settles into an uncomfortably weighted silence, heads shaking back and forth at the tragic comedies we all share.

It took nothing for me to realize how differently the police behaved when the sun and news cameras packed themselves away. It was a joke. I have to repeat that to myself. Somebody probably tweeted it. Somebody else probably laughed. The laughter drifted away as the joke carried itself with startling ease across state lines, following us all north to Minnesota.

The van that was once full of strangers deposited me outside of my apartment. I knew part of the world there expected me to carry on as if nothing had happened. It expected me to abandon Ferguson in Ferguson. But back in Minnesota, I found myself curling around the heat of my own anger, watching the snow melt to reveal what was hidden underneath. Everything that happened in Ferguson was not left there because it was not an oddity but the norm. It may have been a malignant tumor, but it came from a cancerous system that made up the entire country. I saw this looking around the state I called home and realized maybe the only punchline to be found was me.

❦

In June of 1981, Black lesbian, mother, warrior, poet, Audre Lorde gave a keynote presentation at the National Women's Student Association (NWSA) Conference in Storrs, Connecticut. During its early years, the conference was protested by women of color for its racism and failure to include them in the conversation. It was in this context that Lorde came to give her keynote presentation, "The Uses of Anger: Women Responding to Racism", which would eventually be included in her 1984 collection *Sister Outsider: Essays and Speeches.*

"Women respond to racism," Lorde began in her keynote, "My response to racism is anger. I have lived with that anger, ignoring it, feeding upon it, learning to use it before it laid my visions to waste, for most of my life. Once I did it in silence, afraid of the weight."

In her keynote, Lorde responded to the early failures of the NWSA and explored the potential of anger as a tool, and her words remain timely. As Lorde then deconstructed the assumptions that anger could only ever be a destructive force, the same could be said of how anger is viewed today. In our world, though, not a single thing escapes racialization and while Lorde directed part of her keynote to white women in the audience, she also addressed the peculiar reality of Black women's anger.

Her words remind me of growing up as a young Black girl in Minnesota, outside of the cities and their suburbs, where anger is neatly packaged away and the phenomenon of Minnesota Nice is inescapable. You know, that supposed default to friendliness and confrontation avoidance that characterizes Minnesotans in particular.

Some people will experience Minnesota Nice in friendly waves and smiles and strangers that are unflinchingly nice. And yet, Black people know Minnesota Nice in the tightened smiles as people pass by before pulling out their phones to call the police. Minnesota Nice is "Black Lives Matter" and "Blessed Ramadan" signs tossed up around a city where Black masjids are bombed and Black Muslim lives are routinely surveilled.

In Minnesota, fear of anger becomes repackaged as a sort of gift, and to be an angry Black girl in Minnesota was to stand in further contrast. To the state, that anger became a plague. A Black girl's anger made fields rot. It made stomachs turn. It made other children cry, rivers freeze, and was so goddamn powerful, everyone figured it was best to rid Black girls of the habit. But, as Lorde cautioned, "My fear of anger taught me nothing. Your fear of anger will teach you nothing, also."

❧

"But anger expressed and translated into action in the service of our vision and our future is a liberation and strengthening act of clarification, for it is in the painful process of this translation that we identify who are our allies with whom we have grave differences, and who are our genuine enemies," Lorde told her audience.

As Lorde identified anger translated into a new language of action, I realize where I came into that for myself. It was November, and December, in Minnesota when my original joke chased me back out onto the streets. I had already been teaching my tongue how to create new sounds in fury, but this was more. This was standing down the winter freeze and creating a thaw. There, with the heat of my own anger, I learned how to reverse the punchline.

❧

Looking back, the eighteen days of the fourth precinct occupation after Minneapolis police murdered Jamar Clark seem like hardly anything. But when those days passed, they seemed to stretch indefinitely into a separate lifetime. Through them, I came to see how violence recreated itself on new soil. I left everything else behind in favor of those strange new days, where I came to see what my anger was capable of.

A white man's rage at the audacity of Black existence was why a Black man died on the sidewalk, but Black women's rage was why the world stopped at all. For those eighteen days, the fourth precinct I camped outside of became its own sort of place halfway between this world and the next. Maybe knowing that is the only way to convey how I came to be throughout it.

"Anger is loaded with information and energy," Lorde said and that was never more clear than in eighteen days that jumble together because I barely slept through them all. The self who first arrived on the corner of James and Plymouth was not the same self who stared down police in their masks of stoicism every night. In the thaw, I saw my birth, and traced it to before the occupation became an occupation; when it was simply a rally of angry people with the same broken strings somewhere inside of their bodies.

There is something a little cruel about remembering your own birth. On one of those nights, I stood outside the vestibule's locked doors with a friend screaming curses caught between languages and cried. I cried because I was angry and wanted to fight the man she was yelling at. I cried because I wanted to fight the world, period.

Maybe this new self's identity won't ever be proven, but anger is information, and it is archival. My birth certificate is scattered up and down the block in wood fire ashes, green marks of paint, the lingering kiss of mace. My social security was sent up with bullets the night a group of men shot up the occupation. But, I can still count each contraction in the steady beat of someone's fist on glass. And before a rally was a rally, or an occupation an occupation, it was there, on a corner freshly barricaded by police tape, that out of a collective anger contained in hushed whispers, I was conceived.

☙

I have always known anger. Now, I have grown enough to shake her hand and name her. She is no longer an ignored acquaintance, because I've come to share some of her most pivotal moments with her. I learned to lay down with her and identify the parts of her laced within myself until we were finally tied together.

"For it is not the anger of Black women which is dripping down over this globe like a diseased liquid. It is not my anger that launches rockets, spends over sixty thousand dollars a second on missiles and other agents of war and death, slaughters children in cities, stockpiles nerve gas and chemical bombs, sodomizes our daughters and our earth," Lorde said.

I see this now.

And sure, my anger is set to destroy, but not the earth. Just the world that corrupted it. My anger is unflinching when she must be, unforgiving in what she has to address, but she is not here to control. She is not the annihilation that Lorde spoke of, the other type of strange anger that is bent on ruling all. She is, instead, "our power to examine and to redefine the terms upon which we will live and work; our power to envision and reconstruct, anger by painful anger, stone upon heavy stone, a future of pollinating difference and the earth to support our choices."

I joke with anger now, sometimes. Watching as terrible news floods and becomes impossible to turn away from, I go back and forth with anger in our new language until I finally have to pause, shake my head, and quietly mutter a single, yet strongly enunciated, "Damn."

Hair

LYNDSEY ELLIS

In the summer of 2001, I chose to go natural for the first time. The decision, I thought, had more to do with preserving the hair I had left than making a political statement. Excessive heat from curling irons, on top of years of relaxers, had caused my ends to thin, and I wanted to do something about it before starting my freshman year in college.

Cheryl, my best friend, was also entering University of Missouri-Columbia, which was two hours outside of our hometown. She liked the idea of going natural and wanted to do it with me. We made a bet that whoever didn't last and returned to the perm first would pay the other's cell phone bill for the remainder of the school year.

I was glad I wasn't alone, but knew Cheryl had it easier. She had fine hair that frizzed in the heat but didn't nap up like the thick tufts covering my scalp. All she had to do was smooth down her sides with a damp brush and pull the rest into a ponytail at the crown of her head.

Me? I had to get radically creative. At the time, I was afraid of dreadlocks, or the idea of trying to maintain them. The only folks I knew who could pull it off were celebrities I'd seen in magazines, or in music videos on television, like Lauryn Hill, Res, Lenny Kravitz, and Whoopi. I didn't know anyone personally who wore them except Cheryl's mother, Ms. Pam. But, like Cheryl, her mother was on the verge of having what was called "good" hair. Even when we saw Ms. Pam at her worst, looking exhausted after working another graveyard shift, her edges were always laid.

Knowing my experience would be drastically different, I went with letting my new growth accumulate the entire summer until I had a tiny afro and cut off my thinning ends. Then, before the semester started, I got braids because I couldn't bear getting used to short hair in public.

Cheryl and I lived in separate dorms, but we were together all the time. We had the same mutual friends. We went to the same parties. We did the same drugs. We talked shit about the same people. We even had a course together. Literature of the African Diaspora. A small class with more women than men, and an almost equal mix of Blacks and whites, which was a rarity at our ultra-white university.

Dr. O, our professor, was a Nigerian man. Tall and lean, with a strong jawline and chestnut brown skin. Dr. O's class exposed us to various Black poets and writers around the world whose works focused on Black expression and race relations. For the first time, I read *Things Fall Apart* by Chinua Achebe, *Sonny's Blues* by James Baldwin, "Recitatif" by Toni Morrison, and several other classic works. Ultimately, that's when I discovered that I too wanted to be a creative writer, although I wasn't ready to have that conversation outside of my head yet.

Cheryl and I—both closemouthed and self-conscious when we weren't partying on nights and weekends—were two of the only three Black women in the class. The other one, Jade, was a lanky, outspoken fair-skinned woman with natural cropped hair who sat in the front center row. Cheryl and I mocked Jade outside of class; we thought she looked like she reeked of incense, read tarot cards as a side hustle, and got dressed in the dark with hand-me-downs from the local Goodwill.

But, Jade knew a lot of history, especially controversial history with dark secrets revealing the depth of racism that shaped the Midwest. A college junior, she'd worked as a campus tour guide for incoming freshmen the previous summer, and she wasn't shy about pointing out local atrocities she'd discovered to our class. One instance, she said, involved Lloyd L. Gaines, a man who'd drawn attention after being denied admission to the University of Missouri-Columbia's law school because he was Black. Gaines's family had been part of the Great Migration and settled in St. Louis from rural Mississippi in the 1920s. There, Gaines flourished academically and later attended Lincoln University, a historically Black college in Jefferson City, Missouri. After graduating, he applied to law school and filed suit when he was rejected. The U.S. Supreme Court ruled in Gaines's favor but while waiting on classes to open, he traveled to Chicago where he disappeared, never to be heard from again.

In 2000, Mizzou's Black Culture Center was named after Gaines to keep his legacy alive. While one of the unproved theories is that Gaines gave up and relocated to Mexico, legend has it that he was murdered by angry white supremacists who buried his bones somewhere on the university's grounds. I remember hearing several accounts from students who claimed they saw Gaines's ghost roaming around campus.

In Dr. O's class, there was also a rambunctious brother we called Wu-Tang. Thick-necked and bowlegged, he was a Hip-Hop head whose headphones complemented the hoodies he donned over his football jersey, and his box braids always looked fresh. Wu-Tang wasn't your everyday jock, though. His conversation was smooth and intelligent. He loved reading, and it showed in his analyses of our reading assignments during class discussions. Many times, from his seat in the back of the room, Wu-Tang would refute or echo Jade's responses to Dr. O's questions. The two of them would publicly face off until the discussion morphed into a semi-heated debate, but by the end of class they'd be laughing and cracking jokes on each other like it was all for sport.

"Bet you they're fucking," Cheryl said to me one day after class.

"Nah," I told her, "they don't seem like each other's type."

"Them be the ones."

"Girl, whatever."

I waved off her assumption. Wu-Tang, I thought, was more inclined to mess around with one of the sorority chicks like Alison who sat cater-corner to Cheryl and me. Alison, or Cool White Girl as we called her, looked like most of the other white girls on campus with her blonde highlights, eye makeup, and flip-flops, but she seemed friendlier without being fake nice. She greeted us in class and even when we crossed paths on campus. She also wasn't afraid to challenge Jade or Wu-Tang in a class discussion.

One day, Dr. O. asked the class to think of a time when someone around us gave life to a misconception about a different race or culture. It seemed like a packed question that would lead to many interesting answers by those crazy enough to respond. Gradually, people spit out their answers. Alison raised her hand. When Dr. O. called on her, she opened her mouth but nothing came out. Her hands, I noticed, were clutching the sides of her desk. Knuckles so white, they looked like naked bone instead of skin. Dr. O., a patient man, slowly nodded his head, as if to encourage Alison's attempt to find words. Red splotches broke across her face. I thought she was going to cry. Instead, she coughed and ran her hands through her hair.

"My grandmother..." she began.

Alison revealed how her grandmother would take her and her siblings to the movies when they were young kids and warn them not to let their heads touch the theater seats if they didn't want to get cooties from the Blacks. Listening to her, I felt something drop in me that I hadn't known I'd been carrying. Alison must've felt something, too, because she sat forward and slumped over her desk as the rest of the room splintered with tension.

"Man, fuck that."

Wu-Tang and several other Black young men in the back of the room took turns shouting foul comments. Dr. O. let them. I looked at Jade. She seemed unfazed as she picked at her nails. Her back was stiff against her chair, like she'd heard it all before. Like she was determined not to slouch under the weight in the room. Jade had always irked me, but in that moment, I hated her for how she carried on in the face of such an ugly revelation. I hated her even more than I was embarrassed for Alison. I hated her because as much as I didn't want to admit it then, she was teaching me what Black resilience looked like.

❧

After Alison's confession, I didn't use hair grease for a week. Every time I looked at the jars of moisturizer that left my braids smelling good and kept my scalp dandruff-free, I saw Alison as a small child, surrounded by her siblings and her grandmother, each of them making an effort to hold their heads away from the theater's seats as they stared at the movie screen.

"Girl, fuck them," Cheryl told me one day. "You keep that shit up, and you'll be walking around with lice, just like some of them."

But, Cheryl started wearing more hats, I noticed. And, we both avoided movie theaters during our downtime, which wasn't too hard since we were broke college kids who preferred to watch episodes of *Elimidate* and *Cheaters* in the dorms anyway. Cheryl's roommate, Nancy, often went with us on our joyrides in the woods where we smoked weed and listened to chopped and screwed rap music. She was a half Japanese, half Caucasian, and 100% country girl who was from a little town in the Missouri Bootheel. I trusted her, but after what Alison said in class that day, I started watching the way Nancy hit the blunt after one of us passed it to her. Was she letting the swisher paper touch her mouth? Or, with the caution of a subtle racist, did she use her thumb and forearms as a buffer to separate it from her lips?

Truth was, I could never really tell with Nancy, but my attempted observations made me more wary of others in our community as well. How did the non-Black cashiers in grocery stores and gas stations respond to me? Did they let their fingers touch mine when they handed back my change? Or, were they inclined to drop loose coins onto the counter, determined not to make close contact with a Black person? Once, I witnessed a white woman refuse to use the toilet in a public restroom behind me. I washed my hands longer than usual and watched her through the mirror as she waited for another stall to become vacant—

one that had been occupied by another white person.

"You're going to drive yourself nuts if that's all you ever think about," Ms. Dottie, my beautician, warned me. I'd given up on the braids that were supposed to support me while I was growing out my natural hair and during spring break, returned to St. Louis for the first perm I'd had in months. Part of me felt weak and defeated for going back to relaxed hair, but the constant paranoia of being seen as inferior and dirty after Alison's testimony in Dr. O's class wasn't getting any easier to handle. The only thing that comforted me was the fact that I outlasted Cheryl who'd broke down and permed her own hair before college midterms. That, and having Ms. Dottie to confide in about whites' micro-aggressions on campus.

"You been scratching?" she asked. She stirred the white solution in the jar on her counter. "We ran out of 7-Up, so you better brace yourself. Try to keep this in as long as you can."

And, I did. By the time I got to the shampoo bowl, my head was an invisible flame. Tears stung my eyes as Ms. Dottie washed out the relaxer. Wet hair clung to the open wounds on my scalp. The strong, eggy smell of sulfur made my stomach churn.

I grit my teeth, waiting to feel acceptably clean again.

V.
ONWARD

What, what am I to do with all this life?
—Gwendolyn Brooks

(Born in Topeka, Kansas, 1917; Raised in Chicago, Illinois)

Stop Pretending Black Midwesterners Don't Exist

TAMARA WINFREY-HARRIS

I am a Black woman born and raised in the space between the coasts and above the Mason-Dixon line. I am a face of the heartland, but you might not know it if you've been following the Trump-era reporting and commentary about the lives and political choices of people in the Midwest.

After the 2016 election, it was common to hear musings about how Midwestern voters flocked to Donald Trump because he spoke to the America they wanted to make "great"—a descriptor that many argued was code for "white." Richard C. Longworth said in a representative *Guardian* op-ed that Midwestern voters liked Mr. Trump because he articulated their resentment of elites, trade, immigrants, and the Clintons.

That kind of thinking has persisted. "Democrats, nationally, have not had a message or policies that have really connected with Midwestern voters, and that's why we have lost elections here in recent years," Paul Davis, a candidate in the Democratic primary for the House of Representatives in Kansas' Second District, told Reuters in April. The revived sitcom *Roseanne*, before ABC canceled it in response to a racist tirade by its star, was heralded for the way the white family at its center gave voice to the "authentic" Midwestern working-class experience.

These are all reminders that in the minds of many Americans, the region where I have lived all my life is synonymous with whiteness. Of course, that's false. Approximately seven million people who identify as African-American live in the Midwest. That means there are more Black people in the Midwest than in the Northeast or the West. Indiana alone was home to more than 60 Black settlements before the Civil War. Most of us are products of the Great Migration, the exodus of some six million Black Americans from the South from 1916 to 1970. We came here to work, drawn by the industry of the Midwestern Rust Belt. We came here for equal opportunity.

It is a bitter irony, then, that many of the arguments about Mr. Trump's appeal to Midwesterners make sense only if you pretend Black people don't exist in the middle of the country. We are told that economic anxiety, not a willingness to embrace racist rhetoric and policies, drove the white workers of Ohio, Michigan and Wisconsin to cast their lot with Mr. Trump. But what about the profound economic insecurity of their Black counterparts, a vast majority of whom were unwilling to bet on the promises of a David Duke-endorsed candidate to bring the local factory back? A majority of white voters in Ohio, Michigan and Wisconsin chose Donald Trump (62 percent, 57 percent and 53 percent, respectively), while only 6 percent to 8 percent of their Black neighbors did.

Accepting the economic anxiety narrative doesn't only keep us from interrogating the extent to which white citizens of this country are comfortable with—or even energized by—racism. It also erases the contributions of a significant portion of the American work force. My maternal grandfather was among the more than one million Black migrants to the Chicago metropolitan area, attracted by the steel mills that give the South Shore of Lake Michigan its distinctive skyline. With a 10th-grade education, he followed his brothers and sisters north from rural Alabama and found a job. After working at Inland Steel for more than 40 years, he retired with a pension, having purchased a neat little bungalow and having sent three of four children to college.

In my hometown, Gary, Indiana, in the 1960s, you could graduate from high school on Friday and be employed at U.S. Steel by the following Monday. My father, a school administrator and Mississippi transplant who sometimes worked at the mill in the summer, says of the time, "If you didn't have a job, you didn't want a job." This reality dissolved along with the steel industry. U.S. Steel Gary Works employed some 30,000 people in the 1970s; by 2015, it employed around 5,000.

The people in Gary, which is more than 80 percent Black, and in Detroit, another predominantly Black city, where millions of Black Southern migrants once thrived making America's convertibles and Coupe de Villes, are rendered invisible by the country's racially biased understanding of the Midwest and the working class.

The so-called flyover states have long been an avatar for the real America—small towns, country music, conservatism, casseroles and amber waves of grain. Whiteness. It is that mythologized heartland that pundits seem to think will engender empathy, not the Black families of Milwaukee; the majority-Latino community of Dodge City, Kansas; the Burmese Chin refugees of Indianapolis; or the strong Arab community of metropolitan Detroit.

Black workers in the Midwest are as much victims of the postindustrial age as are white Ohio coal miners. Indeed, they may be feeling a deeper ache. Black workers with high school diplomas make less than white workers with the same education; the Black poverty rate is higher; and the median wealth of white households is 10 times that of Black households. The political emphasis on aggrieved white men implies that some families deserve economic stability more than others.

It is not just the white working class that is suffering—it is the working class, period. And we can't solve the problem if we refuse to see who those workers actually are. By 2032, according to the Economic Policy Institute, the American working class will be made up mostly of people of color, including Black workers.

As midterm elections and their accompanying political commentary approach, understanding America and its challenges requires seeing both the working class and Black America in their fullness and recognizing where they intersect. It requires acknowledging the experiences of Black Midwesterners, even when this means adding unflattering nuance to the stories we've long been told about their white neighbors. Because without centuries of economic and cultural contributions from Black people in flyover states, America would not be America at all.

Originally published in The New York Times, *June 16, 2018.*

A Reflection on the Changing Route Work of Sumpter's South End

EZEKIEL JOUBERT III

Sumpter Township's Seal, Courtesy of Janeau Joubert 2018.

I grew up South of Belleville Lake and Interstate 94, a little over thirty miles west of Detroit and about twenty miles east of Ann Arbor, in a rural town of about 9500 residents called Sumpter. The town's geography is defined by the routes of revolutionary soldiers and the migrations of white immigrants, the formerly enslaved, and Black American migrants from the South and Detroit. I often reflect on my lived experiences in and relationships to the rural communities tucked away in the wetlands of the Huron River, at the periphery of Southeast Michigan's industrial rust belt. The short drive through Sumpter exemplifies *you-blink-and-miss-it*, and the lack of streetlights might make it hard for you to navigate at night on the unpaved and sidewalk-less dirt roads—way out in the boonies. Not known for any name-brand products or famous people, just *Country Living at its Finest*, Sumpter Township, Michigan is a homeplace for those folks who yearn for peace and quiet and a connection to and dependence on rural labor and life. While deindustrialization has affected employment and large farms in the area, Sumpter still thrives on its dedication to resisting suburban and urban development.

As a pre-teen, I remember being conflicted about my parents' decision to move from suburban Ann Arbor to rural Sumpter. I saw myself as a city kid and Sumpter as stuck in the past, rooted in a vision I had yet to understand. Those of us who grew up below Judd Road, in what our elders call the "South End," learned to embody a sense of Northern mobility and Southern self-determination. In the predominantly Black part of town—entangled with Deep North segregation and Down South values—our elders forged a space for current and retired Black union auto workers from Ford Motor Company's post-industrial dispossessed cities like Detroit and Inkster and displaced rural workers from the South. With aims to define their own political economy and a connection to their Southern roots, the story of Black folks of Sumpter's South End is one of cooperation and justice. As an educator and community-engaged scholar, their stories have become an essential source of my pedagogical engagement and social commitments. I choose to center the lessons I have learned and continue to gain from the South End and recognize that the knowledges and practices developed there are invaluable to historical discourse and contemporary material questions of Black folks living in rural spaces across the Midwest.

My parents, Ezekiel Jr. and Abishag, who spent their summers in rural Louisiana as children with their grandparents, wanted to share their passion for rural life and its lessons with their children, relatives, and friends. In the warm months, we completed yard work before play: gardening, cutting grass, and cleaning the small barn for our two horses. My brothers Batiste and Janeau and I and youth in our community played organized sports on the cement basketball court my grandfather poured and finished—a skill he mastered in his thirty-eight years as a cement finisher at Ford. When we were not doing chores, playing sports or reuniting with family, we were learning how to, what Paulo Freire calls, "read the world" through the riding lessons we gained by trading our labor, cleaning barns and tending to ponies and goats, with Daryl Phillips, a family friend, organic intellectual and proud Black Horseman. His lessons always included the complex history of the Black Midwest and the importance of literacy to expand our political thought and collective practice. For example, as a teen, he guided me through the imaginary worlds of Toni Morrison and William Shakespeare. The support, generosity and love of engaged community members provided various pathways for learning and development.

My family built a home in the South End during the mid-1990s, on a little over four acres of land my grandparents, Ezekiel Sr. and Josephine, had acquired from a cousin. Like most Black people in town, we belonged to one of the small Black churches, chosen based on Christian denomination and pastoral leadership. At First Missionary Baptist of Belleville, we participated in a variety of youth activities. I sang in the youth choir and later found my passion as a junior Sunday School teacher, where it was prophesied and established that I would one day become an educator. Under the guidance of this community space, we visited the Charles H. Wright Museum of African American History in Detroit and were accustomed to participating in summer camps at Sumpter's Progressive Civic League. The camps were organized as a direct response to the splitting of Sumpter's school districts, which over the years led Black children to attend schools different than the ones some of their neighbors attended. The camp organizers aimed to not only provide academic enrichment, but also worked diligently to help us build community with one another.

My educational research asks how history and the political economy shape the living and educational experiences in rural communities in the Black Midwest. I am drawn to the notions of moving and place-making as ways to explore the relationship between Black education, space, struggle and resistance. The history of Sumpter's South End reveals the socio-politics and cultural expressions of Black American migrants and their praxis. Paul Gilroy, author of *The Black Atlantic: Modernity and Double Consciousness*, describes these visions, theories and practices of knowing, being, and doing as *route work*. Lately, I have reflected deeply on the enclosures of community space in Sumpter, specifically those that affect Black social mobility and community. During my recent visits home, I saw shuttered Black institutions, all of which were vibrant and energetic during my youth. The buildings that housed the Sumpter Progressive Civic League, a historically Black led organization and Mt. Hermon Baptist Church have been demolished. Nate Barnes' Market, a Black owned grocery, eatery, and landmark is no longer there to supply organic produce and meat as it once did. A common place for weekend gatherings and entertainment, Freeman's Hunting and Social Club no longer provides a space for *the blues* and sport. In addition to the dispossession of spaces of Black social life, it is important to note that in 2013, Elwell

Elementary School, the last public educational institution in Sumpter, was forced to close its doors. At the time, the school's minority enrollment was above the state average with a significant black student body.

This history is captured in the lives of Black residents in Sumpter's South End, particularly the young people. Despite the dispossession of collective space, their route work remains rooted in movement and rural place-making. In what follows, I share the route work of three young adult residents who live and work in Sumpter. As a counter-story to the perceptions of rural life in America's "Heartland," these brief profiles express their cultural work and critical thought. What I present demonstrates how they bridge their cultural practices of past with the social challenges of present as a route for imagining a just future in Sumpter's South End.

Britney Vawters' Route Work as a Speculative Fiction

Britney is a queer disabled community-engaged speculative fiction writer. The daughter of former auto worker and Township Supervisor Johnny Vawters, her route work focuses on Black women's identity development, spaces of disinvestment, and queer romantic invisibility. In the speculative world of her online-self-published work *The Detroiter,* she invites us into the inner thoughts and cultural spaces of a queer Black Creole woman journalist Shauna, born and raised in Detroit and living in London. Drawing from her own migration experiences from downriver Detroit to Sumpter and being in a disabled queer body, she explores the contradictions of leaving/escaping home and the weight of loving someone in a trans-species body (werewolf hybrid). Since returning to South End, Britney volunteers with elders at the Sumpter Community Center as a way to gain a historical understanding of lived experiences of Black women from Sumpter, some of who organized with the Sumpter Young Women's Association, a group comprised of young Black women activists. In her books *Everybody's Got Their Something* and *A Sinner's Bible*, Britney gives voice to the unheard and oppressed by lifting up a black woman's point of view to story what it means to *be* in love and to be loved, regardless of flaws and self-doubt and what it means to heal in world that only sees the suffering of Black women and girls. She sees her writing as a tool for shedding light on the often-concealed lives of Black folks whose gender, queerness and blackness are experienced in the margins of Midwest rurality and thus, hopes these stories and her own embodiments can be used to help young black rural queers struggling with invisibility.

Jamarrea Bishop's Route Work as Place-Making

Jamarrea Bishop in his work space (2018), Jungle House (2016) courtesy of Ezekiel Joubert III

Jamarrea is a father, self-taught artist and organic intellectual. His architectural models represent the complex and sometimes contradictory relationships between Black life at the intersections between urban and rural, the African American diaspora, and post-war Black liberation thought. Constructed out of found and natural materials from his family's land, the small-scale structures offer critical insights into questions about the perpetual dispossession of Black rural land and knowledge, both in the past and the present. Like his grandfather Nate Barnes, the first Black business owner in Sumpter, and mother Sheena Barnes, a community leader and artist, his work expresses the long history of self-determined place-making in Sumpter's South End. In the piece he calls "Jungle House," Jamarrea expresses his passion for African history and rural life. He constructs a homeplace in Africa that conveys, through the symbolism of a black eagle's head and helmet structure, in his words, the abundance of *knowledge* and *power* Black people throughout the diaspora possess. He demonstrates in this work and others that despite being from the jungle (or a rural space), we are actively engaging in the production of knowledge, even though no one *sees* us. His fantasy clubhouses act as vessels for imagining a utopian vision for Black life, one in which we creatively transform the places where we live and learn.

Batiste Joubert's Route Work as Ecological Justice

Batiste Joubert at the 5th Annual Eze-J Ranch Trail Ride (2018), Courtesy of Boone Nguyen.

Similar to the visions of Britney and Jamarrea, Batiste's route work as an intergenerational auto worker, horse trainer, riding instructor and father is grounded in preserving relationships to and an understanding of social space. He teaches children and adults how to ride horses by using the practices passed down to him by Black Horsemen in Sumpter. While these practices drive his cultural work, he also aims to combine them with efforts to trace the current ecological needs of the South End community. On horseback, traveling along the roads of Black owned land, he observes, much like a critical geographer, how many of Wayne County's drainage ditches are full of debris and pollution, thus not allowing the water to flow off the land. Following in the Black organizing traditions of Sumpter's South End Concerned Citizens— whose organizing and protest forced Waste Management, Inc. to terminate the use of the landfill in the South End—he believes that the future of land use and development in Sumpter should interrogate the continuing effects of living in proximity to a landfill. From an ecological justice and sustainability perspective, he noticed that the water draining from the landfill floods the South End and raises the water table, making it difficult to build homes and to farm. His goals are to develop eco-initiatives that would bring awareness to the environmental struggles facing young families across the South End.

The South End was, and still is to a degree, comprised of Black-led institutions with community aims for organizing and bringing together the multiplicity of rural knowledge and resources for negotiating and navigating the essential questions of living in rural Midwest in the twenty-first century, including changing land use policies, the effects of proximate suburbanization/rural gentrification, continuous educational redistricting and school closures, growing racial inequality and the inevitability of class struggle. The brief profiles above highlight a few perspectives and approaches from the young people who choose to make Sumpter's South End their home. With mass media and national political discourse constructing rural places as aging, white, poor, and miseducated, their stories disrupt master narratives that erase and exclude rural Black Americans. Their approaches to life and visions for the future, provide insights into the material questions and lives of those affected by structures of race, class, and gender that create hurdles for Black rural life in the Midwest. Their dedication to the social, cultural, and educational development of others and themselves is inspiring and demands attention from political stakeholders and cultural workers whose resources and access is predominantly designated within the boundaries of metropolitan centers. So, as I drive past fields of corn along Midwestern highways, I critically reflect on the Black life being lived in small communities. I treasure the rootedness and route work I have witnessed and imagine, through my work and the work of those profiled above, the possibility and potential for a future in these often-forgotten places.

4 Malcolm X Greenhouse

JORDAN WEBER

How do we live independently of a Midwest system that is unsustainable for our societal whole and live towards communal Black empowerment? If a legacy of violence against the land threatens violence against the bodies that should be nourished and supported by it, how can we best respond? When heritage speaks to survival despite ongoing structural disadvantage, and when legacy is a reminder that lives are surrounded by poisoned lands and bodies, what wisdom compels us to build art objects, now, that our descendants can thrive from?

4 Malcom X Greenhouse (4MX) is a sculptural and programmatic artwork built from an ideation of individual and community holistic health. It promotes, via its own formulations, what I believe to be Malcolm X's greatest contribution as an agent of social change in America: that of self-empowerment. A greenhouse mimicking the shape of Malcolm X's birth house was built on his birth site's land at the

Malcolm X Birth Site Foundation. It is located in North Omaha, a neighborhood with a long history of poverty and social and economic challenges that are defined by racial boundaries, poisoned industrial lands, and food desertification.

4MX acts as a utilitarian art object. Using social practices, it joins those living in a poverty-stricken neighborhood to collectively open the landscape for a healthy Black urbanism. 4MX is a means of action and knowledge within an architectural complex that can be modified for the needs of the Black community. It is an alternative to what can be built within oppressive constructs while challenging the very identity of environment through creative practice. It draws us toward future constructs where art and acting upon one's immediate environment are common practice for new sustainable Midwest societies.

Programs include production of food crops, medicinal herbs, methods of distributing and using these products within the community, and a 'front porch' stage with an adjacent concrete patio for performances and for spiritual and meditation practices. Additionally, partnering local organizations provide programming to assist in soil and home lead clean up, gardening practices, social gatherings, Salah Prayer sessions (facing Mecca), and Zazen mediation classes.

The shape of the greenhouse, that of a single-family residence typical of Malcolm X's birth home, underpins critical questioning. It operates through popular symbology where a house represents safety, independence, and financial accomplishment. Lastly, the porch offers seventeen-acre views of Black-owned landscapes for contemplative and decompression periods, just as it suggests a beacon of fellowship and congregation. However, it does not rest on nostalgic formulations. It asks what sacrifices are required to pursue the Midwest American Dream, typified by land ownership, while being Black in America.

the only moving thing

KISHA NICOLE FOSTER

in chaos
the only thing moving
is what doesn't speak
what sweats and keeps talking
keep it together
keep it one hundred
keep it positive
on the ones and twos

it takes time to unlearn
show patience
stop gossiping
start learning
put the telephone down
youtube cress welsing
feed the brain

thought never stops in sleep
it becomes a nineties punk band
asks us to not snore
wants to push out
hate and name calling and curses
wants the word to be in one book
its in tens of thousands tho
meditating is praying
washing dishes is worshipping
tithing is buying breakfast for a friend
giving your last twenty believing it will
come back

ten fold
ten four
tin foil

tin lizzie
the only moving thing in war and now
is hate and supremacy and we cant keep gasping
our plans behind blank pages
without italics and vegetables
part vegan, pescatarian
craving steak during cycle
the only moving thing at all times are my feet
my heart it beats to the drums in africa
I have love for everyone
just more for my black self
my black daughter my black sun
is in the sky
black bird sings nina simone
my pupils collaged paper as tears
you see me sad
only moving the thing is my tongue
clicking the roof of my mouth where
pyramids look rough and rouge
only the moving thing
should be your heart beating
empathy clasping
loving yourself
then someone named another

we speak our thoughts about race
a psychological dis ease that has people acting unjust
acting ignorant, wailing in our sleep
REM flutters the mind and dream occurs
this is where your mind advances
the thing only moving when all else stops
is the cat that licks its paw on the corner stoop
under the stars Sirius A and B invisible
gaining blue black force: Digitaria.

there is a history that is growing more
red. more hateful. smiles are slithered
slanted to give the illusion of kind.
absolute energy will let you know

we just need to breath and let correct
fill our veins. let it sit there. cease.
wrap yourself around a street pole
place your ear to the sidewalk
let the bloodied pavement serenade names
place your palm on a tree bark
let the nectar of black bodies drizzle fingers

in a room full of sheep and standstill people
be the voice that asks luxurious questions
body suffocated with rugged answers
allow voice to serenade the only moving thing
that stands up for those that are muted by brutal
morph into the checks and balances
that have disappeared with the detained children

the only moving thing that matters
is time.
don't stick.
become unhinged and daring
embody revolution
knowledge the self
free your dome for freedom

if you see a black bird
in a frame
surrounded by opaque
struggle singing
for air to breathe
because most times
it cannot
please
give yourself permission
I beg you
to be
the only moving thing that is not full of fear.

Toward a Black Chicago Revival

MARY PATTILLO

Chicago lost more Black people from 1980 to 2016 (357,387) than live in the city of Washington DC (333,496) (Scarborough et al. 2020). But in 2018, 830,650 Black people still called Chicago home. That number is second only to New York City, and greater than the Black populations of the cities of Atlanta, St. Louis, and Los Angeles, combined.* That's a lot of Black people. That's why Chicago is still a Black Metropolis (Drake and Cayton 2015).

Of course numbers alone don't make Black Chicago a Black Metropolis. That distinction comes from the 78,010 Black-owned businesses in Chicago (U.S. Census Bureau 2012); 18 (out of 50) Black Aldermen/women and dozens of state and U.S. representatives; 395 Black churches;† 305 majority Black public schools (Chicago Public Schools 2018); 40 chapters of Black Greek-Letter organizations in the Chicago's Pan-Hellenic Council (and the national headquarters of Alpha Kappa Alpha sorority); 4 Predominately Black institutions of higher education; 2 Black-owned radio stations; 1 Black bank; the annual Bud Billiken Day Parade; public housing reunion picnics despite the buildings being demolished over a decade ago (Bowean 2019; Hunter et al. 2016); and around 24,000 Twitter followers each for @AssataDaughters and @BLMChi, 212,000 (and counting) for @eveewing, and 8.2 million for Black Chicago hometown hero @chancetherapper. And, of course, let's not forget the Black Mayor and Black Cook County Board president.

With the constant barrage of bad news—the Chiraq label, Trump's targeted attacks, the perennial top 5 ranking for racial residential segregation, the selling of *The Chicago Defender*, *Ebony* and *Jet* (still to Black owners,

---

*According to the 2018 U.S. Census population estimates for the respective cities, available at https://data.census.gov/: Atlanta: 261,747; Los Angeles 396,416; St. Louis 142,596. All of these figures refer to the "Black alone or combination" numbers, and include Black Hispanics.

 This is the tally for Black Protestant Congregations in Cook County (Grammich et al 2018), which is of course larger than the City of Chicago, but excludes Black Catholic congregations, which number roughly 29 in Chicago according to http://www.usccb.org/issues-and-action/cultural-diversity/african-american/demographics/parishes-with-a-strong-black-catholic-presence.cfm, and Black Muslim mosques.

just not Chicago-based), 563 murders in 2018, and Black population decline, just to name a few—it is not easy to celebrate Black Chicago, especially without sounding blind to the real hardships and suffering that many Black Chicagoans endure. But just as Robert Abbott called for the Great Northern Drive in 1917, in a racial atmosphere combustible enough to spark the 1919 Race Riots just a few years later, we still can and must be boosters of Black Chicago despite its defects (Ewing 2019).

The rationale for insisting on a *Black Chicago Revival* is to counter countercyclical Black migration patterns such that "black and white population change are inversely correlated" (Scarborough et al. 2019, p. 33). A repeated story of Black migration is arriving a day late and a dollar short. Black folks arrived in northern cities in the second wave of the Great Migration just as urban deindustrialization was dawning (Sugrue 2014). Factories were falling apart after wartime production and looking to rebuild anew in the suburbs and overseas. Accordingly, White suburbanization took off in the 1950s, while Black suburbanization lagged more than twenty years behind, picking up just as the suburban housing stock was aging and the inner-ring suburbs in particular were shedding jobs. Now, White people are moving back to the city, and Black people are moving out.

Of course it is not by happenstance that Black people's moves have been too late to take advantage of the most plentiful opportunities and investments. Instead, Black people have been systematically excluded from advantageous places, until we push our way in; once we do, White people (supported by governments, employers, real estate professionals, and others) often take their spoils and move elsewhere. Calling for a Black Chicago Revival is about standing our ground as the city becomes prime real estate again. It is about recognizing these racist cycles of possession and dispossession, hoarding and exclusion, exodus and return, and intervening through Black creativity, demand, and rootedness.

Black creativity refers not just to the arts—although that is surely a part of it—but rather to the creation of a future Black Chicago that arrests the conditions of unemployment, school closures, over-policing, substandard health care, environmental pollution, and other maladies. Black creativity is manifest in the plethora of Black service-providers, teachers, investors, coaches, ministers, mentors, neighborhood moms/ dads/elders, philanthropists, advocates, gardeners and farmers, block club members, and political activists—working both within Black organizations and with collaborators—to heal wounds and cultivate assets so that Black Chicago can flourish. Black people do this work wherever we live (Hunter 2013). Doing it in Chicago builds on the legacy of previous generations of Black Chicagoans, and refuses to let the fruits of that labor be capitalized upon without Black people's participation and cultural, spiritual, and economic profit.

Many of the same people and organizations that are being creative are also undertaking the important work of Black *demand*. The lie of White wealth and advantage is that it is totally self-generated. The reality is that the public and private sectors have greased the wheels of White success. Black demand is about recognizing this centuries-long history, and redressing it with investments that benefit Black Chicagoans. A recent report on housing discrimination in Chicago found that "between 75 percent and 95 percent of the homes sold to black families during the 1950s and '60s were sold on contract… The amount of wealth land sales contracts expropriated from Chicago's black community was between 3.2 and 4.0 billion dollars" (Cook Center on Social Equity 2019, iii). The authors continue: "contract selling enjoyed the backing of the very banks that turned down black homebuyers and of investment syndicates comprised of white Chicago lawyers, doctors, downtown business leaders, and city government officials, all of whom profited handsomely by exploiting a separate and unequal housing market to the profound disadvantage of black families" (ii). Those actors owe Black Chicagoans for that plunder, both in the form of monetary reparations and preferential access to opportunities that enhance wealth and well-being.

Finally, Black rootedness. While being "stuck" in disadvantaged places has had negative repercussions for generations of Black people (Sharkey 2013), staying in a place as it improves is a good thing. The problem is, just as places starts to get better, Black people get the boot. $1.7 billion in Chicago city government investments is concentrated "where gentrification has resulted in a decline in the black population and an increase in the white population" (Scarborough 2020, p. 50). This suggests that Black erasure is a pre-requisite for White investment (Fullilove 2004). Countering the forces of Black removal is not at all easy, but making visible the cycle is the first step to insisting on policies and efforts that protect Black people and Black neighborhoods. Such policies include affordable housing preservation and construction, property tax relief, community land trusts, emergency rental assistance, community benefits agreements, rent control, and preferential housing vouchers, among other things. But these are stopgap measures for when a neighborhood gets hot. What's also needed are ongoing and robust pre-hot-market public investments in schools, parks, libraries, health centers, air quality, food systems, and the arts, particularly where families are least able to pay for these things privately. Such improvements will allow Black families who want to stay rooted to do so.

These investments are the anchors of healthy places, and putting them where Black people already are—rather than driving people away in search of them, or providing them once Black people have left—requires the combination of Black creativity, demand, and rootedness. Black population loss in Chicago has not occurred in a historical or structural vacuum. Interrupting these forces requires acknowledging the racist cycles of urban change and committing to new ways of operating that recognize the profound value and mighty presence of Black Chicago.

This essay is a revised version of "Black Chicago Ain't Dead," first published as a commentary to the 2020 report "Between the Great Migration and Growing Exodus: The Future of Black Chicago?" published by the Institute for Research on Race and Public Policy at the University of Illinois at Chicago.

References

Bowean, Lolly. Sept. 6, 2019. "For former Chicago public housing residents, the complexes are gone but their sense of community remains." *Chicago Tribune* (Online).

Chicago Public Schools. 2018. Racial/Ethnic Report: School Year 2018-2019.https://cps.edu/Performance/Documents/DataFiles/Demographics_RacialEthnic_2019.xls

Cook (Samuel DuBois) Center on Social Equity. 2019. *The Plunder of Black Wealth in Chicago.* Duke University. https://socialequity.duke.edu/sites/socialequity.duke.edu/files/The%20Plunder%20of%20Black%20Wealth%20in%20Chicago.pdf

Drake, St. Clair, and Horace R. Cayton. 2015. *Black Metropolis: a Study of Negro life in a Northern City.* Chicago: University of Chicago Press.

Ewing, Eve. 2019. *1919.* Chicago: Haymarket Books.

Fullilove, Mindy. 2004. *Root Shock.* New York: One World/Ballantine Books.

Grammich, Clifford, Kirk Hadaway, Richard Houseal, Dale E. Jones, Alexei Krindatch, Richie Stanley, and Richard H. Taylor. 2018. U.S. Religion Census: Religious Congregations and Membership Study, 2010 (County File). http://www.thearda.com/Archive/Files/Descriptions/RCMSCY10.asp

Hunter, Marcus Anthony. 2013. *Black Citymakers: How The Philadelphia Negro Changed Urban America.* New York: Oxford University Press.

Hunter, Marcus Anthony, Mary Pattillo, Zandria F. Robinson, and Keeanga-Yamahtta Taylor. 2016. "Black Placemaking: Celebration, play, and poetry." *Theory, Culture & Society* 33: 31-56.

Scarborough, William, Iván Arenas, and Amanda E. Lewis. 2020. "Between the Great Migration and Growing Exodus: The Future of Black Chicago?" Chicago. Institute for Research on Race and Public Policy, University of Illinois at Chicago. https://irrpp.uic.edu/pdf/publications/IRRPP_StateOfRacialJustice_FutureOfBlackChicago.pdf

Sharkey, Patrick. 2013. *Stuck in Place: Urban Neighborhoods and the End of Progress toward Racial Equality.* Chicago: University of Chicago Press.

Sugrue, Thomas J. 2014. *The Origins of the Urban Crisis: Race and Inequality in Postwar Detroit.* Updated Edition. Princeton, NJ: Princeton University Press.

U.S. Census Bureau 2012. 2012 Survey of Business Owners. Table: Statistics for All U.S. Firms by Industry, Gender, Ethnicity, and Race for the U.S., States, Metro Areas, Counties, and Places. https://factfinder.census.gov/faces/tableservices/jsf/pages/productview.xhtml?pid=SBO_2012_00CSA01&prodType=table.

Infinite Essence: James, 2018

MIKAEL CHUKWUMA OWUNNA

"Infinite Essence" is my response to pervasive media images of black people dead and dying. Being gunned down by police officers, drowning and washing up on the shores of the Mediterranean, starving and suffering in award-winning photography. The trope of the black body as a site of death is everywhere.

What if the only images you saw of people who looked like you were dead and dying bodies? How would that affect the way you move through the world, how would that enter (and hamper) your body?

With this series, I've set about on a quest to recast the black body as the cosmos and eternal. I hand paint all of the models' bodies with fluorescent paints, and using my engineering background I have built my own flash to only pass ultraviolet light. Using this method, in total darkness, I click down on the shutter—"snap"—and for a fraction of a second, their bodies illuminate as the universe. We view the beauty of the soul and our deeper cosmic connections communicated through them.

In Igbo spirituality, odinani, we believe in the existence of a "chi" in every person. Ultraviolet light is not visible to the human eye, and so we can illuminate and find—albeit temporarily—the unseeable therein, the soul, the chi. It is on this plane of existence where, regardless of our experiences of oppression on the physical plane, we are infinite.

Coda: A Final Note on Black Life and Loss

I submitted the full draft of *Black in the Middle* to Dan Crissman, my editor at Belt, in mid-February 2020. Just a few weeks later, the ground would shift under my feet and the feet of the entire nation when the coronavirus pandemic forced most of us into a kind of surreal pseudo-hibernation that completely upended the way we do business—and life in general. Very quickly commonplace things like face masks, toilet paper, and hand sanitizer became prized possessions, even as terms like "social distancing" and "flattening the curve" and "personal protective equipment" became part of our everyday lexicon.

Who could have imagined, then, that the ground could, and would, shift even more dramatically just a couple of months later? The killing of forty-six-year-old George Floyd on May 25 by Derek Chauvin and three of Chauvin's colleagues from the Minneapolis Police Department only compounded the tensions of many black people, who were already contending with the disparate effects of the pandemic on themselves, their families, and their communities. In Minneapolis, where the Black Midwest Initiative is based, the death of *one more* unarmed black person at the hands of law enforcement in the context of *one more* national crisis that had become so heavy a burden for black people to bear erupted into a local rebellion that soon became national and then worldwide in scope.

Though we never could have anticipated the moment in which *Black in the Middle* would appear, I think I can probably speak for many if not most of the book's contributors when I say I'm not at all surprised that the Midwest would become the epicenter of the latest racial upheaval. Part of what this collection endeavors to do is reckon with the routinized brutalities and systemic inequalities that have historically structured, and continue to structure, so much of black Midwestern life—and which far too few people recognized as the kindling for both the actual and metaphorical fires that were set in the Twin Cities in late May.

But, notice, there is yet another call to which we respond. In 1988, Toni Morrison gave a commencement address at Sarah Lawrence College during which she called on the graduates to "dream the world as it ought to be, imagine what it would feel like not to be living in a world loaded with zero-life weapons manned by people willing to loose them, develop them, or store them for money, or power, or data, but never for your life and never for mine." In times such as these, when our rage and fear and pain have been sutured to, seemingly, every waking moment of our lives, we cannot afford to discontinue dreaming. While "the world as it ought to be" might feel like an impossibly distant future, it is what we are doing here, together, now, that will sustain us into the alternative possibilities we dream up by way of our writing, our poetry, our art, our music, our dancing, our gathering, our love.

Terrion
June 2020

The Black Midwest: A Bibliography
Compiled by the Black Midwest Initiative

For the purposes of this bibliography, the "Midwest" consists of the twelve states designated as part of the Midwest census region by the United States Census Bureau, as well as other heavy manufacturing centers that are typically considered part of the "Rust Belt." The bibliography is not meant to be a compilation of black authors from the Midwest but, rather, identifies books that principally concern black people and are centrally set in the region. It is also a work-in-progress that will be periodically updated on our website. If you have entries to submit, please visit us at theblackmidwest.com.

NONFICTION

Chicago

Absher, Amy. *The Black Musician and the White City: Race and Music in Chicago, 1900-1967*. Ann Arbor: University of Michigan Press, 2014.

Agyepong, Tera Eva. *The Criminalization of Black Children: Race, Gender, and Delinquency in Chicago's Juvenile Justice System, 1899-1945*. Chapel Hill: University of North Carolina Press, 2018.

Alkalimat, Abdul, Romi Crawford, and Rebecca Zorach, eds. *The Wall of Respect: Public Art and Black Liberation in 1960s Chicago*. Evanston, IL: Northwestern University Press, 2017.

Allen, Joe. *People Wasn't Made to Burn: A True Story of Housing, Race, and Murder in Chicago*. Chicago: Haymarket Books, 2011.

Baldwin, Davarian L. *Chicago's New Negroes: Modernity, the Great Migration, and Black Urban Life*. Chapel Hill: University of North Carolina Press, 2007.

Balto, Simon. *Occupied Territory: Policing Black Chicago from Red Summer to Black Power*. Chapel Hill: University of North Carolina Press, 2019.

Bates, Beth Tompkins. *Pullman Porters and the Rise of Protest Politics in Black America, 1925-1945*. Chapel Hill: University of North Carolina Press, 2001.

Black Jr., Timuel D. *Bridges of Memory: Chicago's First Generation of Black Migration*. Evanston, IL: Northwestern University Press, 2005.

—. *Bridges of Memory: Chicago's Second Generation of Black Migration*. Evanston, IL: Northwestern University Press, 2008.

Blair, Cynthia M. *I've Got to Make My Livin': Black Women's Sex Work in Turn-of-the Century Chicago*. Chicago: University of Chicago Press, 2010.

Bone, Robert and Richard A. Courage. *The Muse in Bronzeville: African American Creative Expression in Chicago, 1932-1950*. New Brunswick, NJ: Rutgers University Press, 2011.

Boyd, Michelle R. *Jim Crow Nostalgia: Reconstructing Race in Bronzeville*. Minneapolis: University of Minnesota Press, 2008.

Cain, Mary Ann. *South Side Venus: The Legacy of Margaret Burroughs*. Evanston, IL: Northwestern University Press, 2018.

Chaskin, Robert J. and Mark L. Joseph. *Integrating the Inner City: The Promise and Perils of Mixed-Income Public Housing Transformation*. Chicago: University of Chicago Press, 2015.

Chatelain, Marcia. *South Side Girls: Growing Up in the Great Migration*. Durham, NC: Duke University Press, 2015.

Deppe, Martin L. *Operation Breadbasket: An Untold Story of Civil Rights in Chicago, 1966-1971*. Athens: University of Georgia Press, 2017.

Diamond, Andrew J. *Chicago on the Make: Power and Inequality in a Modern City*. Oakland: University of California Press, 2017.

Dolinar, Brian, ed. *The Negro in Illinois: The WPA Papers*. Urbana: University of Illinois Press, 2013.

Drake, St. Clair. *Black Metropolis: A Study of Negro Life in a Northern City*. Chicago: University of Chicago Press, 1945.

Duneier, Mitchell. *Slim's Table: Race, Respectability, and Masculinity*. Chicago: University of Chicago Press, 1992.

Ewing, Eve L. *Ghosts in the Schoolyard: Racism and School Closings on Chicago's South Side*. Chicago: University of Chicago Press, 2018.

Finley, Mary Lou, Bernard LaFayeette Jr., James R. Ralph Jr., and Pam Smith. *The Chicago Freedom Movement: Martin Luther King Jr. and Civil Rights Activism in the North*. Lexington: University Press of Kentucky, 2016.

Garb, Margaret. *Freedom's Ballot: African American Political Struggles in Chicago from Abolition to the Great Migration*. Chicago: University of Chicago Press, 2014.

Green, Adam. *Selling the Race: Culture, Community, and Black Chicago, 1940-1955*. Chicago: University of Chicago Press, 2007.

Grimshaw, William J. *Bitter Fruit: Black Politics and the Chicago Machine, 1931-1991*. Chicago: University of Chicago Press, 1992.

Grossman, James R. *Land of Hope: Chicago, Black Southerners, and the Great Migration*. Chicago: University of Chicago Press, 1989.

Hancock, Black Hawk. *American Allegory: Lindy Hop and the Racial Imagination.* Chicago: University of Chicago Press, 2013.

Hayner, Don. *Binga: The Rise and Fall of Chicago's First Black Banker.* Evanston: Northwestern University Press, 2019.

Helgeson, Jeffrey. *Crucibles of Black Empowerment: Chicago's Neighborhood Politics from the New Deal to Harold Washington.* Chicago: University of Chicago Press, 2014.

Hine, Darlene Clark and John McCluskey Jr., eds. *The Black Chicago Renaissance.* Urbana: University of Illinois Press, 2012.

Hirsch, Arnold R. *Making the Second Ghetto: Race & Housing in Chicago, 1940-1960.* Chicago: University of Chicago Press, 1983.

Hunt, D. Bradford. *Blueprint for Disaster: The Unraveling of Chicago Public Housing.* Chicago: University of Chicago Press, 2009.

Kimble Jr., Lionel. *A New Deal for Bronzeville: Housing, Employment & Civil Rights in Black Chicago, 1935-1955.* Carbondale: Southern Illinois University Press, 2015.

Kotlowitz, Alex. *An American Summer: Love and Death in Chicago.* New York: Doubleday, 2019.

—. *There Are No Children Here: The Story of Two Boys Growing Up in the Other America.* New York: Anchor Books, 1991.

Knupfer, Anne Meis. *The Chicago Black Renaissance and Women's Activism.* Urbana: University of Illinois Press, 2006.

Levin, Josh. *The Queen: The Forgotten Life Behind an American Myth.* New York: Little, Brown and Company, 2019.

McCammack, Brian. *Landscapes of Hope: Nature and the Great Migration in Chicago.* Cambridge, MA: Harvard University Press, 2017.

Michaeli, Ethan. *The Defender: How the Legendary Black Newspaper Changed America.* New York: Houghton Mifflin Harcourt Publishing, 2016.

Moore, Natalie Y. *The South Side: A Portrait of Chicago and American Segregation.* New York: St. Martin's Press, 2016.

Mullen, Bill V. *Popular Fronts: Chicago and African-American Cultural Politics, 1935-46.* University of Illinois Press, 1999.

Mumford, Kevin J. *Interzones: Black/White Sex Districts in Chicago and New York in the Early Twentieth Century.* New York: Columbia University Press, 1997.

Pattillo, Mary. *Black on the Block: The Politics of Race and Class in the City.* Chicago: University of Chicago Press, 2008.

—. *Black Picket Fences: Privilege and Peril Among the Black Middle Class.* 2nd ed. Chicago: University of Chicago Press, 2013.

Petty, Audrey, ed. *High Rise Stories: Voices from Chicago Public Housing*. San Francisco: McSweeney's Books, 2013.

Pruter, Robert. *Chicago Soul*. Champaign: University of Illinois Press, 1991.

—. *Doowop: The Chicago Scene*. Champaign: University of Illinois Press, 1996.

Ralph, James. *Northern Protest: Martin Luther King, Jr., Chicago, and the Civil Rights Movement*. Cambridge, MA: Harvard University Press, 1993.

Ralph, Laurence. *Renegade Dreams: Living Through Injury in Gangland Chicago*. Chicago: University of Chicago Press, 2014.

Reed, Christopher Robert. *"All the World Is Here!": The Black Presence at White City*. Bloomington: Indiana University Press, 2000.

—. *The Chicago NAACP and the Rise of Black Professional Leadership, 1910-1966*. Bloomington: Indiana University Press, 1997.

Sandburg, Carl. *The Chicago Race Riots: July, 1919*. New York: Harcourt, Brace, and Howe, 1919.

Scarborough, William, Iván Arenas, and Amanda E. Lewis. "Between the Great Migration and Growing Exodus: The Future of Black Chicago?" Institute for Research on Race and Public Policy. University of Illinois at Chicago, 2020. Available at irrpp.uic.edu.

Seligman, Amanda I. *Block by Block: Neighborhoods and Public Policy on Chicago's West Side*. Chicago: University of Chicago Press, 2005.

Shabazz, Rashad. *Spatializing Blackness: Architectures of Confinement and Black Masculinity in Chicago*. Urbana: University of Illinois Press, 2015.

Spear, Allan H. *Black Chicago: The Making of a Negro Ghetto, 1890-1920*. Chicago: University of Chicago Press, 1967.

Travis, Dempsey. *An Autobiography of Black Chicago*. Chicago: Agate Bolden, 1981.

Tuttle, Jr. *Race Riot: Chicago in the Red Summer of 1919*. New York: Atheneum, 1970.

Venkatesh, Sudhir Alladi. *American Project: The Rise and Fall of a Modern Ghetto*. Cambridge, MA: Harvard University Press, 2000.

—. *Off the Books: The Underground Economy of the Urban Poor*. Cambridge, MA: Harvard University Press, 2006.

Weems Jr., Robert E. and Jason P. Chambers. Eds. *Building the Black Metropolis: African American Entrepreneurship in Chicago*. Urbana: University of Illinois Press, 2017.

Williams, Jakobi. *From the Bullet to the Ballot: The Illinois Chapter of the Black Panther Party and Racial Coalitional Politics in Chicago*. Chapel Hill: University of North Carolina Press, 2013.

Young, Jr. Alford A. *The Minds of Marginalized Black Men: Making Sense of Mobility, Opportunity, and Future Life Chances*. Princeton, NJ: Princeton University Press, 2004.

Zorach, Rebecca. *Art for People's Sake: Artists and Community in Black Chicago, 1965-1975*. Durham, NC: Duke University Press, 2019.

Detroit

Bailey, Marlon M. *Butch Queens Up in Pumps: Gender, Performance, and Ballroom Culture in Detroit*. Ann Arbor: University of Michigan Press, 2013.

Bates, Beth Tompkins. *The Making of Black Detroit in the Age of Henry Ford*. Chapel Hill: University of North Carolina Press, 2012.

Bergmann, Luke. *Getting Ghost: Two Young Lives and the Struggle for the Soul of an American City*. New York: The New Press, 2008.

Bjorn, Lars. *Before Motown: A History of Jazz in Detroit, 1920-1960*. Ann Arbor: University of Michigan Press, 2001.

Boggs, James. *The American Revolution: Pages from a Negro Worker's Notebook*. New York: Monthly Review Press, 1963.

Boyd, Herb. *Black Detroit: A People's History of Self-Determination*. New York: HarperCollins, 2017.

Boyd, Melba Joyce. *Wresting with the Muse: Dudley Randall and the Broadside Press*. New York: Columbia University Press, 2003.

Boyle, Kevin. *Arc of Justice: A Saga of Race, Civil Rights, and Murder in the Jazz Age*. New York: Henry Holt and Company, 2004.

Bridge Magazine and The Detroit Journalism Cooperative. *The Intersection: What Detroit Has Gained, and Lost, 50 Years After the Uprisings of 1967*. Traverse City, MI: Mission Point Press, 2017.

Cox, Aimee Meredith. *Shapeshifters: Black Girls and the Choreography of Citizenship*. Durham, NC: Duke University Press, 2015.

Darden, Joe T., Richard Child Hill, June Thomas, and Richard Thomas. *Detroit: Race and Uneven Development*. Philadelphia: Temple University Press, 1987.

Early, Gerald. *One Nation Under a Groove: Motown and American Culture*. New York: Ecco Press, 1995.

Fine, Sidney. *Violence in the Model City: The Cavanagh Administration, Race Relations, and the Detroit Riot of 1967*. East Lansing: Michigan State University Press, 2007.

Georgakas, George and Marvin Surkin. *Detroit: I Do Mind Dying: A Study in Urban Revolution*. 3rd ed. Chicago: Haymarket Books, 2012.

Hamera, Judith. *Unfinished Business: Michael Jackson, Detroit, and the Figural Economy of American Deindustrialization*. New York: Oxford University Press, 2017.

Hersey, John. *The Algiers Motel Incident*. Baltimore: Johns Hopkins University Press, 1968.

Kinney, Rebecca J. *Beautiful Wasteland: The Rise of Detroit as America's Postindustrial Frontier*. Minneapolis: University of Minnesota Press, 2016.

Kurashige, Scott. *The Fifty-Year Rebellion: How the U.S Political Crisis Began in Detroit*. Oakland: University of California Press, 2017.

Lewis-Colman, David M. *Race Against Liberalism: Black Workers and the UAW in Detroit*. Urbana: University of Illinois Press, 2008.

Locke, Herbert G. *The Detroit Riot of 1967*. Detroit: Wayne State University Press, 1969.

Meier, August and Elliott Rudwick. *Black Detroit and the Rise of the UAW*. Oxford University Press, 1979.

Miles, Tiya. *The Dawn of Detroit: A Chronicle of Slavery and Freedom in the City of the Straits*. New York: The New Press, 2017.

Moon, Elaine Latzman. *Untold Tales, Unsung Heroes: An Oral History of Detroit's African American Community, 1918-1967*. Detroit: Wayne State University Press, 1993.

Rich, Wilbur C. *Coleman Young and Detroit Politics: From Social Activist to Power Broker*. Detroit: Wayne State University Press, 1989.

Robinson, Julia Marie. *Race, Religion, and the Pulpit: Rev. Robert L. Bradby and the Making of Urban Detroit*. Detroit: Wayne State University Press, 2015.

Smith, Suzanne E. *Dancing in the Street: Motown and the Cultural Politics of Detroit*. Cambridge, MA: Harvard University Press, 1999.

Stone, Joel, ed. *Detroit 1967: Origins, Impacts, Legacies*. Detroit: Wayne State University Press, 2017.

Sugrue, Thomas J. *The Origins of the Urban Crisis: Race and Inequality in Postwar Detroit*. Princeton: Princeton University Press, 1996.

Thompson, Heather Ann. *Whose Detroit? Politics, Labor, and Race in a Modern American City*. Ithaca, NY: Cornell University Press, 2001.

Thompson, Julius E. *Dudley Randall, Broadside Press, and the Black Arts Movement in Detroit, 1960-1995*. Jefferson, NC: McFarland, 2005.

Triece, Mary E. *Urban Renewal and Resistance: Race, Space, and the City in the Late Twentieth to Early Twenty-First Century*. Lanham, MD: Lexington Books, 2016.

Williams, Jeremy. *Detroit: The Black Bottom Community*. Charleston, SC: Arcadia Publishing, 2009.

Wolcott, Victoria W. *Remaking Respectability: African American Women in Interwar Detroit*. Chapel Hill, NC: University of North Carolina Press, 2001.

Illinois (other than Chicago)

Barr, Mary. *Friends Disappear: The Battle for Racial Equality in Evanston*. Chicago: University of Chicago Press, 2014.

Cha-Jua, Sundiata Keita. *America's First Black Town: Brooklyn, Illinois, 1830-1915*. Champaign: University of Illinois Press, 2000.

Fleisher Mark S. *Living Black: Social Life in an African American Neighborhood*. Madison: University of Wisconsin Press, 2015.

Hamer, Jennifer. *Abandoned in the Heartland: Work, Family, and Living in East St. Louis*. Berkeley: University of California Press, 2011.

Hendricks, Wanda A. *Gender, Race, and Politics in the Midwest: Black Club Women in Illinois*. Bloomington: Indiana University Press, 1998.

Lumpkins, Charles L. *American Pogrom: The East St. Louis Race Riot and Black Politics*. Athens: Ohio University Press, 2008.

Turner, Glennette Tilly. *The Underground Railroad in Illinois*. Newman Educational Publishing, 2001.

Williamson, Joy Ann. *Black Power on Campus: The University of Illinois, 1965-75*. Champaign: University of Illinois, 2003.

Williamson, Terrion L. *Scandalize My Name: Black Feminist Practice and the Making of Black Social Life*. New York: Fordham University Press, 2017.

Indiana

Barnes, Sandra L. *The Cost of Being Poor: A Comparative Study of Life in Poor Urban Neighborhoods in Gary, Indiana*. Albany: State University of New York Press, Albany, 2005.

Bigham, Darrel E. *We Only Ask a Fair Trial: A History of the Black Community in Evansville, Indiana*. Bloomington: Indiana University Press, 1987.

Carr, Cynthia. *Our Town: A Heartland Lynching, a Haunted Town, and the Hidden History of White America.* New York: Three Rivers Press, 2006.

Debono, Paul. *The Indianapolis ABCs: History of a Premier Team in the Negro Leagues.* Jefferson, NC: McFarland & Company, 2007.

Lassiter, Luke Eric, Hurley Goodall, Elizabeth Campbell, and Michelle Natasya Johnson. *The Other Side of Middletown: Exploring Muncie's African American Community.* Walnut Creek, CA: AltaMira Press, 2004.

Madison, James H. *A Lynching in the Heartland: Race and Memory in America.* New York: Palgrave Macmillan, 2001.

Pearsey, Patrick R. *Guardians of the Avenue: African-American Officers with the Indianapolis Police Department.* 2017.

—. *Guardians of the Avenue 2: Biographies of African-American Legends of the Indianapolis Police Department.* 2017.

Pierce, Richard B. *Polite Protest: The Political Economy of Race in Indianapolis, 1920-1970.* Bloomington, IN: Indiana University Press, 2005.

Robinson, Gabrielle. *Better Homes of South Bend: An American Story of Courage.* Charleston, SC: The History Press, 2015.

Thornbrough, Emma Lou. *Indiana Blacks in the Twentieth Century.* Bloomington, IN: Indiana University Press, 2000.

—. *The Negro in Indiana before 1900: A Study of a Minority.* Bloomington, IN: Indiana University Press, 1993.

Vincent, Stephen A. *Southern Seed, Northern Soil: African-American Farm Communities in the Midwest, 1765-1900.* Bloomington: Indiana University Press, 1999.

Wallis, Don. *All We Had Was Each Other: The Black Community of Madison, Indiana.* Bloomington: Indiana University Press, 1998.

Williams, Gregory Howard. *Life on the Color Line: The True Story of a White Boy Who Discovered He Was Black.* New York: Plume, 1996.

Iowa

Barnes, Charlene J. and Floyd Bumpers. *Iowa's Black Legacy.* Chicago: Arcadia Publishing, 2000.

Chase, Rachelle. *Creating the Black Utopia of Buxton, Iowa.* Charleston, SC: The History Press, 2019.

—. *Lost Buxton.* Charleston, SC: Arcadia Press, 2017.

Dykstra, Robert R. *Bright Radical Star: Black Freedom and White Supremacy on the Hawkeye Frontier.* Cambridge, MA: Harvard University Press, 1993.

Gradwohl, David M. and Nancy M. Osborn. *Buxton: Work and Racial Equality in a Coal Mining Community.* Ames: Iowa State University Press, 1987.

—. *Exploring Buried Buxton: Archaeology of an Abandoned Iowa Coal Mining Town with a Large Black Population.* Iowa City: University of Iowa Press, 1990.

Gutsche, Jr., Robert E. *A Transplanted Chicago: Race, Place and the Press in Iowa City.* Jefferson, NC: McFarland, 2014.

Hill, Lena M. and Michael D. Hill. *Invisible Hawkeyes: African Americans at the University of Iowa during the Long Civil Rights Era.* Iowa City: University of Iowa Press, 2016.

Parker, Honesty. *African Americans of Des Moines and Polk County.* Charleston, SC: Arcadia Publishing, 2011.

Schweider, Dorothy, Joseph Hraba, and Elmer Schweider. *Buxton: A Black Utopia in the Heartland.* Iowa City: University of Iowa Press, 2003.

Soike, Lowell J. *Necessary Courage: Iowa's Underground Railroad in the Struggle against Slavery.* Iowa City: University of Iowa Press, 2013.

Kansas

Athearn, Robert G. *In Search of Canaan: Black Migration to Kansas, 1879-80.* Lawrence: Regents Press of Kansas, 1978.

Campney, Brent M. S. *This Is Not Dixie: Racist Violence in Kansas, 1861-1927.* Urbana: University of Illinois Press, 2015.

Cunningham, Roger D. *The Black Citizen-Soldiers of Kansas, 1864-1901.* Columbia: University of Missouri Press, 2008.

Painter, Nell Irvin. *Exodusters: Black Migration to Kansas after Reconstruction.* New York: Alfred A. Knopf, 1977.

Spurgeon, Ian Michael. *Soldiers in the Army of Freedom: The 1st Kansas Colored, the Civil War's First African American Combat Unit.* Norman: University of Oklahoma Press, 2014.

Warren, Kim Cary. *The Quest for Citizenship: African American and Native American Education in Kansas, 1880-1935.* Chapel Hill: University of North Carolina Press, 2010.

Michigan (other than Detroit)

Clark, Anna. *The Poisoned City: Flint's Water and the American Urban Tragedy*. New York: Metropolitan Books, 2018.

Cox. Anna-Lisa. *A Stronger Kinship: One Town's Extraordinary Story of Hope and Faith*. New York: Little, Brown and Company, 2006.

Hammond, Rose Louise. *Idlewild and Woodland Park, Michigan: An African American Remembers*. Run With It, 1994.

Highsmith, Andrew R. *Demolition Means Progress: Flint, Michigan and the Fate of the American Metropolis*. Chicago: University of Chicago Press, 2015.

Stephens, Ronald J. *Idlewild: The Black Eden of Michigan*. Chicago: Arcadia Publishing, 2001.

—. *Idlewild: The Rise, Decline, and Rebirth of a Unique African American Resort Town*. Ann Arbor: University of Michigan Press, 2013.

Walker, Lewis and Ben C. Wilson. *Black Eden: The Idlewild Community*. East Lansing: Michigan State University Press, 2002.

Midwest/Rust Belt Region

Blocker, Jack S. *A Little More Freedom: African Americans Enter the Urban Midwest, 1860-1930*. Athens: Ohio State University Press, 2008.

Cox, Anna-Lisa. *The Bone and Sinew of the Land: America's Forgotten Black Pioneers and the Struggle for Equality*. New York: Hachette, 2018.

Glasrud, Bruce A. and Charles A. Braithwaite, eds. *African Americans on the Great Plains: An Anthology*. Lincoln: University of Nebraska Press, 2009.

Hagedorn, Ann. *Beyond the River: The Untold Story of the Heroes of the Underground Railroad*. New York: Simon & Schuster, 2002.

Lehman, Christopher P. *Slavery in the Upper Mississippi Valley, 1787-1865: A History of Human Bondage in Illinois, Iowa, Minnesota and Wisconsin*. Jefferson, NC: McFarland & Company, 2011.

Schwalm, Leslie A. *Emancipation's Diaspora: Race and Reconstruction in the Upper Midwest*. Chapel Hill: University of North Carolina Press, 2000.

Suggs, Henry Lewis. *The Black Press in the Middle West, 1865-1985*. Westport, CT: Greenwood Press, 1996.

Minnesota

Cavett, Kate. *Voices of Rondo: Oral Histories of St. Paul's Historic Black Community*. Minneapolis: Syren Book Company, 2005.

Fairbanks, Evelyn. *The Days of Rondo: A Warm Reminiscence of St. Paul's Thriving Black Community in the 1930s and 1940s*. St. Paul: Minnesota Historical Society Press, 1990.

Fedo, Michael. *The Lynchings in Duluth*. St. Paul: Minnesota Historical Society Press, 1979.

Glanton, John. *Double Exposure: Images of Black Minnesota in the 1940s*. St. Paul: Minnesota Historical Society Press, 2018.

Green, William D. *A Peculiar Imbalance: The Fall and Rise of Racial Equality in Minnesota, 1837-1869*. Minneapolis: University of Minnesota Press, 2015.

—. *Degrees of Freedom: The Origins of Civil Rights in Minnesota, 1865-1912*. Minneapolis: University of Minnesota Press, 2015.

Ibrahim, Hudda. *From Somalia to Snow: How Central Minnesota Became Home to Somalis*. Edina, MN: Beaver's Pond Press, 2017.

Lehman, Christopher P. *Slavery's Reach: Southern Slaveholders in the North Star State*. St. Paul: Minnesota Historical Society Press, 2019.

Swensson, Andrea. *Got to Be Something Here: The Rise of the Minneapolis Sound*. Minneapolis: University of Minnesota Press, 2017.

Taylor, David Vassar. *African Americans in Minnesota*. St. Paul: Minnesota Historical Society Press, 2002.

White, Frank M. *They Played for the Love of the Game: Untold Stories of Black Baseball in Minnesota*. St. Paul: Minnesota Historical Society Press, 2016.

Yusef, Ahmed Ismail. *Somalis in Minnesota*. St. Paul: Minnesota Historical Society Press, 2012.

Missouri

Burke, Diane Mutti. *On Slavery's Border: Missouri's Small Slaveholding Households, 1815-1865*. Athens: University of Georgia Press, 2010.

Early, Gerald, ed. *"Ain't But a Place": An Anthology of African American Writings about St. Louis*. Missouri Historical Society Press, 1999.

Ervin, Keona K. *Gateway to Equality: Black Women and the Struggle for Economic Justice in St. Louis*. Lexington: The University Press of Kentucky, 2017.

Frazier, Harriet C. *Lynchings in Missouri, 1803-1981*. Jefferson, NC: McFarland, 2009.

Gordon, Colin. *Citizen Brown: Race, Democracy, and Inequality in the St. Louis Suburbs*. Chicago: University of Chicago Press, 2019.

Jack, Bryan M. *The St. Louis African American Community and the Exodusters*. Columbia: University of Missouri Press, 2007.

Johnson, Walter. *The Broken Heart of America: St. Louis and the Violent History of the United States*. New York: Basic Books, 2020.

Jolly, Kenneth S. *Black Liberation in the Midwest: The Struggle in St. Louis, Missouri, 1964-1970*. New York: Routledge, 2006.

Ladner, Joyce. *Tomorrow's Tomorrow: The Black Woman*. 1971.

Lang, Clarence. *Grassroots at the Gateway: Class Politics and Black Freedom Struggle in St. Louis, 1936-75*. Ann Arbor: University of Michigan Press, 2009.

Lawrence, David Todd and Elaine J. Lawless. *When They Blew the Levee: Race, Politics, and Community in Pinhook, Missouri*. Jackson: University Press of Mississippi, 2018.

Norwood, Kimberly Jade, ed. *Ferguson's Fault Lines: The Race Quake that Rocked a Nation*. Chicago: American Bar Association, 2016.

Prince, Vida "Sister" Goldman. *That's the Way It Was: Stories of Struggle, Survival and Self-Respect in Twentieth-Century Black St. Louis*. Charleston, SC: The History Press, 2013.

Rogers, Jamala. *Ferguson is America: Roots of Rebellion*. St. Louis: Mira Digital Publishing, 2015.

Smith, Jeff. *Ferguson in Black and White*. Kindle, 2014.

Wright Sr., John A. *Kinloch: Missouri's First All Black Town*. Chicago: Arcadia Publishing, 2000.

—. *St. Louis: Disappearing Black Communities*. Charleston, SC: Arcadia Publishing, 2004.

—. *The Ville: St. Louis*. Chicago: Arcadia Publishing, 2001.

Nebraska

Forss, Amy Helene. *Black Print with a White Carnation: Mildred Brown and the* Omaha Star *Newspaper, 1938-1989*. Lincoln: University of Nebraska Press, 2013.

Holland, Matt. *Ahead of Their Time: The Story of the Omaha Deporres Club*. North Charleston, NC: CreateSpace, 2014.

Marantz, Steve. *The Rhythm Boys of Omaha Central: High School Basketball at the '68 Racial Divide*. Lincoln: University of Nebraska Press, 2011.

New York (Western)

Kraus, Neil. *Race, Neighborhoods, and Community Power: Buffalo Politics, 1934-1997*. Albany: State University of New York Press, 2000.

Overacker, Ingrid. *The African American Church Community in Rochester, New York, 1900-1940*. Rochester: University of Rochester Press, 1998.

Williams, Lillian Serece. *Strangers in the Land of Paradise: The Creation of an African American Community, Buffalo, New York, 1900-1940*. Bloomington: Indiana University Press, 1999.

North Dakota

Dunkel, Tom. *Color Blind: The Forgotten Team That Broke Baseball's Color Line*. New York: Grove Press, 2013.

Newgard, Thomas P., William C. Sherman, and John Guerrero. *African Americans in North Dakota: Sources and Assessments*. 1994.

Ohio

Alkalimat, Abdul and Rubin Patterson, eds. *Black Toledo: A Documentary History of the African American Experience in Toledo, Ohio*. Chicago: Haymarket Books, 2019.

Bigham, Darrel E. *On Jordan's Banks: Emancipation and Its Aftermath in the Ohio River Valley*. Lexington: University Press of Kentucky, 2006.

Griffin, William W. *African Americans and the Color Line in Ohio, 1915-1930*. Athens: Ohio State University Press, 2017.

Griffler, Keith P. *Front Line of Freedom: African Americans and the Forging of the Underground Railroad in the Ohio Valley*. Lexington: University Press of Kentucky, 2004.

Kusmer, Kenneth L. *A Ghetto Takes Shape: Black Cleveland, 1870-1930*. Urbana: University of Illinois Press, 1978.

Michney, Todd M. *Surrogate Suburbs: Black Upward Mobility and Neighborhood Change in Cleveland, 1900-1980*. Chapel Hill: University of North Carolina Press, 2017.

Middleton, Stephen. *The Black Laws: Race and the Legal Process in Early Ohio*. Athens: Ohio University Press, 2005.

Moore, Dan Méndez. *Six Days in Cincinnati: A Graphic Account of the Riots That Shook the Nation a Decade Before Black Lives Matter*. Portland, OR: Microcosm Publishing, 2017.

Phillips, Kimberley L. *AlabamaNorth: African-American Migrants, Community, and Working-Class Activism in Cleveland, 1915-45*. Urbana: University of Illinois Press, 1999.

Stradling, David. *Where the River Burned: Carl Stokes and the Struggle to Save Cleveland*. Ithaca, NY: Cornell University Press, 2015.

Taylor, Nikki M. *Driven Toward Madness: The Fugitive Slave Margaret Garner and Tragedy on the Ohio*. Athens: Ohio University Press, 2016.

—. *Frontiers of Freedom: Cincinnati's Black Community, 1802-1868*. Athens: Ohio University Press, 2005.

VanHorne-Lane, Janice. *Safe Houses and the Underground Railroad in East Central Ohio*. Charleston, SC: The History Press, 2010.

Pennsylvania (Western)

Brewer Jr., John M. *African Americans in Pittsburgh*. Charleston, SC: Arcadia Publishing, 2006.

Crouch, Stanley. *One Shot Harris: The Photographs of Charles "Teenie" Harris*. New York: Abrams, 2002.

Dickerson, Dennis C. *Out of the Crucible: Black Steel Workers in Western Pennsylvania, 1875-1980*. Albany: State University of New York Press, 1986.

Finley, Cheryl, Laurence Glasco, and Joe W. Trotter. *Teenie Harris Photographer: Image, Memory, History*. Pittsburgh: University of Pittsburgh Press, 2011.

Frazier, LaToya Ruby. *The Notion of Family*. New York: Aperture, 2014.

Lester, Larry and Sammy J. Miller. *Black Baseball in Pittsburgh*. Charleston, SC: Arcadia Publishing, 2001.

Trotter Jr. Joe William. And Eric Ledell Smith, eds. *African Americans in Pennsylvania: Shifting Historical Perspectives*. University Park: Pennsylvania State University Press, 1997.

Whitaker, Mark. *Smoketown: The Untold Story of the Other Great Black Renaissance*. New York: Simon & Schuster, 2018.

South Dakota

VanEpps-Taylor, Betti. *Forgotten Lives: African Americans in South Dakota*. Pierre: South Dakota State Historical Society Press, 2008.

Wisconsin

Baker, H. Robert. *The Rescue of Joshua Glover: A Fugitive Slave, the Constitution, and the Coming of the Civil War.* Athens: Ohio University Press, 2006.

Black, Ivory Abena. *Bronzeville: A Milwaukee Lifestyle.* The Publishers Group, 2006.

Cooper, Zachary. *Black Settlers in Rural Wisconsin.* Madison: State Historical Society of Wisconsin, 1977.

Dahlk, Bill. *Against the Wind: African Americans and the Schools in Milwaukee, 1963-2002.* Milwaukee: Marquette University Press, 2010.

Desmond, Matthew. *Evicted: Poverty and Profit in the American City.* New York: Crown, 2016.

Dougherty, Jack. *More Than One Struggle: The Evolution of Black School Reform in Milwaukee.* Chapel Hill: University of North Carolina Press, 2004.

Geenen, Paul H. *Civil Rights Activism in Milwaukee: South Side Struggles in the '60s and '70s.* Charleston, SC: The History Press, 2014.

—. *Milwaukee's Bronzeville, 1900-1950.* Charleston, SC: Arcadia Publishing, 2006.

Jackson, Ruby West and Walter T. McDonald. *Finding Freedom: The Untold Story of Joshua Glover, Runaway Slave.* Madison: State Historical Society of Wisconsin, 2007.

Jones, Patrick D. *The Selma of the North: Civil Rights Insurgency in Milwaukee.* Cambridge. MA: Harvard University Press, 2010.

McManus, Michael J. *Political Abolitionism in Wisconsin, 1840-1861.* Kent, OH: Kent State University Press, 1998.

Mouser, Bruce L. *For Labor, Race, and Liberty: George Edwin Taylor, His Historic Run for the White House, and the Making of Independent Black Politics.* Madison: University of Wisconsin Press, 2011.

Nelsen, James K. *Educating Milwaukee: How One City's History of Segregation and Struggle Shaped Its Schools.* Madison: Wisconsin Historical Society Press, 2015.

Trotter Jr., Joe William. *Black Milwaukee: The Making of an Industrial Proletariat, 1915-45.* 2nd ed. Champaign: University of Illinois Press, 2007.

Witt, Andrew. *The Black Panthers in the Midwest: The Community Programs and Services of the Black Panther Party in Milwaukee, 1966-1977.* New York: Routledge, 2007.

AUTOBIOGRAPHY/MEMOIR/ESSAYS

Black Jr., Timuel D. *Sacred Ground: The Chicago Streets of Timuel Black.* Evanston, IL: Northwestern University Press, 2019.

Cameron, James. *A Time of Terror: A Survivor's Story.* 1982.

Carruthers, Charlene A. *Unapologetic: A Black, Queer, and Feminist Mandate for Radical Movements.* Boston: Beacon Press, 2018.

Carter Jr., Melvin. *Diesel Heart: An Autobiography.* St. Paul: Minnesota Historical Society Press, 2019.

Davis, Bridgett M. *The World According to Fannie Davis: My Mother's Life in the Detroit Numbers.* New York: Little, Brown and Company, 2019.

Dunham, Katherine. *A Touch of Innocence: A Memoir of Childhood.* Chicago: University of Chicago Press, 1959.

Fisher, Antwone Quenton. *Finding Fish: A Memoir.* New York: HarperCollins, 2001.

Ford, Tanisha C. *Dressed in Dreams: A Black Girl's Love Letter to the Power of Fashion.* New York: St. Martin's Press, 2019.

Gartz, Linda: Redlined: *A Memoir of Race, Change, and Fractured Community in 1960s Chicago.* Berkeley, CA: She Writes Press, 2018.

Gibson, Vivian. *The Last Children of Mill Creek.* Cleveland, OH: Belt Publishing, 2020.

Gooch, U. L. 'Rip' with Glen Sharp. *Black Horizons: One Aviator's Experience in the Post-Tuskegee Era.* Newton, KS: CreateSpace, 2015.

Hartfield, Ronne. *Another Way Home: The Tangled Roots of Race in One Chicago Family.* Chicago: University of Chicago Press, 2004.

Jefferson, Margo. *Negroland: A Memoir.* New York: Vintage, 2015.

Johnson, Arthur L. *Race and Remembrance: A Memoir.* Detroit: Wayne State University Press, 2008.

Love, Laura. *You Ain't Got No Easter Clothes: A Memoir.* New York: Hyperion, 2004.

Lyles, Charlise. *Do I Dare Disturb the Universe? From the Projects to Prep School: A Memoir.* Cleveland: Gray & Company, 1994.

McSpadden, Lezley with Lyah Beth LeFlore. *Tell the Truth & Shame the Devil: The Life, Legacy, and Love of My Son Michael Brown.* New York: Regan Arts, 2016.

Parks, Gordon. *A Choice of Weapons.* 1966.

Pate, Alexs, with Pamela R. Fletcher and J. Otis Powell, eds. *Blues Vision: African American Writing from Minnesota.* St. Paul: Minnesota Historical Society Press, 2015.

Smith, Otis Milton and Mary M. Stolberg. *Looking Beyond Race: The Life of Otis Milton Smith*. Detroit: Wayne State University Press, 2000.

Thompson, Era Bell. *American Daughter*. Chicago: University of Chicago Press, 1946.

Walker, Jerald. *Street Shadows: A Memoir of Race, Rebellion, and Redemption*. New York: Bantam Books, 2010.

Wideman, John Edgar. *Brothers and Keepers*. New York: Holt, Rinehart and Winston, 1984.

Young, Coleman and Lonnie Wheeler. *Hard Stuff: The Autobiography of Mayor Coleman Young*. New York: Viking, 1994.

FICTION/DRAMA/POETRY

Brooks, Gwendolyn. *Maud Martha*. New York: Harper & Brothers, 1953.

Brown, Frank London. *Trumbull Park*. Washington, D.C.: Henry Regnery Company, 1959.

Bulawayo, NoViolet. *We Need New Names*. New York: Reagan Books, 2013.

Clair, Maxine. *Rattlebone*. New York: Farrar, Straus and Giroux, 1994.

Cleage, Pearl. *I Wish I Had a Red Dress*. New York: HarperCollins, 2001.

—. *What Looks Like Crazy on an Ordinary Day*. New York: Avon Books, 1997.

Davis, Bridgett M., *Into the Go-Slow*. New York: Feminist Press, 2014.

Farah, Nuruddin. *Crossbones*. New York: Penguin Books, 2011.

Flournoy, Angela. *The Turner House: A Novel*. New York: Houghton Mifflin Harcourt, 2015.

Forrest, Leon. *Divine Days*. New York: W. W. Norton & Company, 1995.

Goodman, Eric. *Twelfth & Race: A Novel*. Lincoln, NE: Bison Books, 2012.

Greenlee, Sam. *The Spook Who Sat by the Door*. 1969.

Hannaham, James. *Delicious Foods: A Novel*. New York: Little Brown and Company, 2016.

Hansberry, Lorraine. *A Raisin in the Sun*. New York: Random House, 1958.

Hughes, Langston. *Not Without Laughter*. New York: Alfred A. Knopf, 1930.

Johnson, Javon and Kevin Coval, eds. *The End of Chiraq: A Literary Mixtape*. Evanston, IL: Northwestern University Press, 2018.

Lauren, E'mon. *Commando*. Chicago: Haymarket Books, 2017.

Lowe, Janice A. *Leaving CLE: Poems of Nomadic Dispersal*. Oxford, OH: Miami University Press, 2016.

Marshall, Nate. *Wild Hundreds*. Pittsburgh: University of Pittsburgh Press, 2015.

Messner, Susan. *Grand River and Joy*. Ann Arbor: University of Michigan Press, 2009.

Morisseau, Dominique. *Detroit '67*. London: Oberon Books, 2013.

Morrison, Toni. *Beloved*. New York: Alfred A. Knopf, 1987.

—. *The Bluest Eye*. New York: Holt, Rinehart, and Winston, 1970.

—. *Song of Solomon*. New York: Alfred A. Knopf, 1977.

—. *Sula*. New York: Alfred A. Knopf, 1973.

Parks, Gordon. *The Learning Tree*. New York: Fawcett Books, 1963.

Pitts, Jr. Leonard. *Grant Park*. Chicago: Agate Bolden, 2015.

Shange, Ntozake. *Betsey Brown*. New York: Picador, 1985.

Tyree, Omar. *Sweet St. Louis*. New York: Simon & Schuster, 1999.

Verdelle, A.J. *The Good Negress: A Novel*. Chapel Hill, NC: Algonquin Books, 1995.

Webster, Chaun. *GeNtry!fication or the Scene of the Crime*. Blacksburg, VA: Noemi Press, 2018.

Wideman, John Edgar. *Damballah*. New York: Houghton Mifflin, 1981.

—. *Hiding Place*. New York: Houghton Mifflin, 1981.

—. *Sent for You Yesterday*. New York: Avon Books, 1983.

—. *Two Cities*. New York: Houghton Mifflin, 1998.

Wilson, August. *Fences*. New York: Plume, 1986.

—. *Gem of the Ocean*. New York: Theatre Communications Group, 2003.

—. *Jitney*. New York: Theatre Communications Group, 2008. Written in 1979.

—. *Joe Turner's Come and Gone*. New York: Plume, 1988.

—. *King Hedley II*. New York: Theatre Communications Group, 1999.

—. *Ma Rainey's Black Bottom*. New York: Plume, 1981.

—. *The Piano Lesson*. New York: Plume, 1990.

—. *Radio Golf*. New York: Theatre Communications Group, 2007.

—. *Seven Guitars*. New York: Plume, 1996.

—. *Two Trains Running*. New York: Plume, 1992.

Wright, Richard. *Native Son*. New York: Harper & Brothers, 1940.

Zoboi, Ibi. *American Street*. New York: HarperCollins, 2017.

Acknowledgments

I must express my gratitude, first and foremost, to all of the contributors whose vision, talent, and abiding commitment to black Midwestern life made this book possible. You are among those people who will help (re-)shape the narratives of this region in the years to come and I am deeply honored that you accepted the call to be part of this project. Thank you as well to all of the people, groups, and organizations who presented at, attended, and supported the event that was the catalyst for this book—the inaugural Black Midwest Initiative symposium, "Black in the Middle," which was held October 17-19, 2019 on the campus of the University of Minnesota, Twin Cities. That special gathering only confirmed for me how powerful, how resilient, and how intensely caring black Midwesterners are and can be. Let's do it again real soon.

All love to the ever so dope members of the Black Midwest Initiative, particularly those who were part of the original coordinating committee that was instrumental in getting the Initiative, and the symposium, off the ground—Rose Brewer, Lauren Eldridge, Tia-Simone Gardner, Jane Henderson, Zenzele Isoke, Ezekiel Joubert, Kidiocus King-Carroll, Rahsaan Mahadeo, Denise Pike, and Chaun Webster. Also, much gratitude to the newer members of the Initiative who will be largely responsible for shepherding our work into the future.

My heartfelt thanks as well to the current and former members of the University of Minnesota community who each stepped up in their own special way to support the work of the Initiative, including Jasmine Baxter, Angela Boutch, Sara Cronquist, Kat Hayes, Karen Ho, Agnes Malika, Kevin Murphy, Tade Okediji, Jennifer Peterson, Christine Powell, Lauren Sietsema, Catherine Squires, Devona Thomas, and Vanessa Steele. Additional thanks go out to the College of Liberal Arts and the faculties and staffs of the African American & African Studies Department, the American Studies Department, the Gender, Women & Sexuality Studies Department, and the Race, Indigeneity, Gender & Sexuality Studies Initiative for their continued support of both me and the Black Midwest Initiative.

A special shout-out to Bella Rolland for so graciously stepping in to help out with organizational details related to the book at the final hour.

You lightened the load when I needed it most and it meant so very much.

Very many thanks also to all of the visionary, hard-working folks at Belt Publishing, especially Dan Crissman, for all they've done to make this book a reality and for all of the work they do every single day to support Midwestern and Rust Belt writing.

Finally, to all of my beloved friends and family members, near and far, who have helped me to stay the course throughout the past few years as I've been working to help the Initiative, the symposium, and the book take root—thank you for answering when I call and for understanding when I don't, for lifting me up when I'm at my best and for refusing to let me fall when I'm at my worst, and for being my deepest inspiration and the greatest source of my strength.

—Terrion L. Williamson

Contributors

Leslie Barlow is a visual artist, educator, and space creator living and working in Minneapolis, MN. Barlow's current artwork uses figurative oil painting to share stories that explore the politics of representation, identity, otherness, and racial constructs. Barlow actively exhibits her work throughout the United States and many of her pieces can be found in private and public collections. In 2019 she was awarded both the McKnight Visual Artist Fellowship and the 20/20 Springboard Fellowship, and in 2020 was a recipient of the MSAB Cultural Community Partnership Grant. She teaches at the University of Minnesota and Carleton College, helps run the organization MidWest Mixed, and she also supports emerging artists as the founder and Program Director of Studio 400.

Joe Boyle teaches American history at Morrison R. Waite High School in Toledo, Ohio. He spent 10 years teaching at Rogers High School, proudly serving the students of Spencer-Sharples. He is a graduate of Bowling Green State University with a B.A. in History and an M.Ed. in Curriculum and Instruction. His essay is adapted from his M.Ed. project.

Gabrielle Civil is a black feminist performance artist, poet, and writer, originally from Detroit, MI. She has premiered fifty performance works around the world and is the author of the performance memoirs *Swallow the Fish* (2017) and *Experiments in Joy* (2019). Her writing has also appeared in *Dancing While Black, Small Axe, Art21, Obsidian, Kitchen Table Translation, New Daughters of Africa* and "Experiments in Joy: a Workbook." A 2019 Rema Hort Mann LA Emerging Artist, she teaches critical studies and creative writing at the California Institute of the Arts. The aim of her work is to open up space.

Tara L. Conley is an assistant professor in the School of Communication and Media at Montclair State University. She was born and raised in Northeast Ohio, where she grew up playing high school basketball and running track. In 1998 she earned the title of Ohio state long jump champion, cementing her legacy in Ohio sports. As a scholar, her research explores the everyday lives of Black people—primarily Black women and girls—in the study and exploration of place, media histories, and technoculture. For more information, visit taralconley.org.

Beverly Cottman is an interdisciplinary artist creating at the intersections of literary, visual, and performance art. As storyteller *Auntie Beverly,* she delivers wisdom of the ages through stories, folktales, and fables rooted in African and African-American traditions. Her storytelling presentations pass on values and celebrate culture. Her workshop sessions support and encourage participants to create compelling narratives that educate, enlighten, and entertain. Beverly's literary works explore the joys of everyday life and express gratitude for the kinship of family and friends. Her creative endeavors are gifts from the ancestors.

Curtis L. Crisler was born and raised in Gary, Indiana. Crisler has five full-length poetry books, two YA books, and five poetry chapbooks. He's been published in a variety of magazines, journals, and anthologies. He's been a contributing poetry editor, and editor. Also, he created the Indiana Chitlin Circuit. Crisler and is an Associate Professor of English at Purdue University Fort Wayne (PFW). He can be contacted at www.poetcrisler.com.

Nia Easley is an artist and designer based in Chicago, IL. She has shown work in the US, Czech Republic, and Switzerland. Recent accomplishments include traveling to Haiti to assist with a design workshop and designing a billboard off of a major expressway in Chicago. She is a vocal proponent of ethics in design practice. You can find Nia's artist's books in the Joan Flasch Artists' Book Collection and Archives at SAIC, the special collections at DePaul University and the University of Iowa, and the artists' book collection at Northwestern University.

Lyndsey Ellis is a fiction writer and essayist who's passionate about intergenerational resilience in the Midwest. She was a recipient of the San Francisco Foundation's Joseph Henry Jackson Literary Award in 2016 and the Money For Women/Barbara Deming Memorial Fund in 2018 for her fiction. Ellis is a 2018-19 Kimbilio Fiction Fellow and the excerpt editor for *The Coil.* Her writing appears in *The Offing, Joyland, Entropy, Shondaland,* and elsewhere.

Aaron K. Foley is a Detroit-based writer. He is the author of *How to Live in Detroit Without Being a Jackass* and the editor of *The Detroit Neighborhood Guidebook.*

Tanisha C. Ford is an award-winning writer, cultural critic, and Professor of History at The Graduate Center, CUNY. She is the author of *Dressed in Dreams: A Black Girl's Love Letter to the Power of Fashion*; *Kwame Brathwaite: Black Is Beautiful*; and *Liberated Threads: Black Women, Style, and the Global Politics of Soul.*

Kisha Nicole Foster is a mother, poet, and an arts administrator. Foster is the recipient of the 2019 Cleveland Arts Prize for Emerging Artist in Literature. She is the author of *Poems: 1999–2014* and *Bloodwork*. Foster is also in her fourth year as Regional Coordinator for Poetry Out Loud, a program of The Poetry Foundation and the National Endowment of the Arts, sponsored through The Ohio Arts Council. She is a two-time Pink Door Fellow, and currently the Literary Cleveland Fellow/Cleveland Stories program coordinator. Foster was commissioned to craft a poem for the Tamir Rice Foundation and their event "Arts, Activism, and Legacy" at the Cleveland Museum of Art, and The Soul of Philanthropy Cleveland Closing Celebration at Rocket Mortgage Fieldhouse. Foster, a senior at Cleveland State University, uses her locution as a conduit towards healing and fostering truth within language. She is a fan of a good documentary.

brian g. gilmore teaches social justice law in the Clinical Law Program at Michigan State University College of Law. He is originally from Washington DC and the author of four collections of poetry, including the latest, *come see about me, marvin* (Wayne State University Press), a Library of Michigan Notable Book for 2020. He is a columnist with The Progressive Media Project (The Progressive—Madison, Wisconsin). His book, *We Didn't Know Any Gangsters*, is a 2014 NAACP Image Award nominee and a 2015 Hurston-Wright Legacy Award nominee.

Devon Ginn (he/him/they/them) is the Visual Art & Entertainment Curator at the historic Madam Walker Legacy Center. Ginn also serves as the Vice President of the board at the Indiana Writers Center and facilitates an inclusive poetry series called Iconoclast. Ginn is an Americans for the Arts 2019-2020 Fellow, an Arts Council of Indianapolis 2020-2021 Creative Renewal Fellow, a placekeeper + placemaker, and a poet. As a freelance teaching artist, Ginn travels from state-to-state implementing his performance poetry and creative writing workshops. Deliberately collaborating with groundbreaking institutions at the forefront of change, his work as a visual artist, writer, nonprofit administrator, and performance artist is a reflection of all his learned and unlearned experiences.

Janice N. Harrington's latest book of poetry is *Primitive: The Art and Life of Horace H. Pippin* (BOA Editions, 2016). She teaches at the University of Illinois, where she is Director of the Creative Writing Program.

Zenzele Isoke is Associate Professor of Gender, Women, and Sexuality Studies at the University of Minnesota. She has lived and worked in the Twin Cities of Minnesota since 2007. She is a twin native of St. Louis, Missouri and Long Beach, California. She is currently completing a political ethnography of the Twin Cities written from the perspective of Black femmes who use collaborative Black artmaking as a political praxis called *Dissenting Lives: Black Femaleness, Racial Justice, Activist Praxis*. Her work has appeared in several peer-reviewed journals, including *Theory & Event, Souls: Journal of Black Politics, Culture & Society, Transforming Anthropology: A Journal of Black Anthropologists* and *Gender, Place & Culture*, among other venues. She is the author of *Urban Black Women and the Politics of Resistance* (Palgrave Macmillan 2013).

Michelle S. Johnson PhD, a public scholar in the fields of Black history, literature and cultural production, extensively secures and promotes intersectional spaces to express autonomy and authenticity. Johnson speaks widely on historic Black experiences in Michigan and collaborates with activists, researchers, local residents, non-profit and museum leaders across the state to generate exhibits, data-bases, websites, historic designations, art installations, archives, performances and curriculums. Co-founder and former Executive Director of Kalamazoo's Fire Historical and Cultural Arts Collaborative, Johnson appears as weekly radio host DJ Disobedience, generates public access through the new Public Scholarship Foundation and her podcast series, Syncopate.

Ezekiel Joubert III is an educator, community engaged scholar, and creative writer. He is an Assistant Professor of Educational Foundations in the Division of Advanced and Applied Studies at California State University-Los Angeles. His scholarship explores the intersections of racial capitalism, student movement, and Black education and the history of educational inequality in Black rural communities near Metro Detroit and in the Midwest.

Kidiocus King-Carroll is a doctoral candidate in the department of American Studies at the University of Minnesota, Twin Cities.

Jamaal May's award-winning books are *Hum* and *The Big Book of Exit Strategies* (Alice James Books, both). Individual poems have appeared in journals in the US and internationally. His multidisciplinary work has been exhibited at the Smithsonian. Jamaal has won awards and fellowships from Lannan Foundation, Civitella Ranieri Foundation, American Library Association, American Academy of Arts and Letters, Bucknell University, and Kenyon College among others. He teaches in Detroit at Wayne State University, where he guides the [re]launch of Organic Weapon Arts as well as the grassroots sonic support outfit, Jamtramck Beat Systems, which provides equipment and other needs to musicians and sound artists in Hamtramck, Detroit, and Highland Park, MI. Jamaal's current research and creative projects involve various genres and research into empathy through shared sensory experience, and experimental literary forms.

Phyllis M. May-Machunda is a 6th generation Black Midwesterner, whose research interests include African American folklore and music traditions, emphasizing artistic traditions of African American women and children in the Midwest and South; and multicultural and social justice education. She earned her Bachelor of Music degree from the University of Iowa; M.A. and Ph.D. in Folklore/Ethnomusicology from Indiana University-Bloomington, and just completed 30 years as Professor of American Multicultural Studies at Minnesota State University Moorhead. She has published articles, curated exhibitions, co-facilitated community-based social justice education programs, and before moving to Minnesota, worked as a folklorist/curator at the Smithsonian Institution.

Edward M. Miggins' world was primarily shaped by Michael and Ann Miggins, his parents who migrated through Ellis Island to NYC in the 1920s. They paid $48 for a rent-controlled apartment in Inwood, Manhattan. He attended Fairfield, Case Western Reserve and Columbia Universities. He became a volunteer in the Catholic Worker in the Bowery and started as a teacher in Spanish Harlem in NYC. He has taught at Cuyahoga Community College and Cleveland State University. He now lives with his family (Janet, Emily and Sarah) in Morro Bay, California.

Gladys Mitchell-Walthour is an Associate Professor of Public Policy & Political Economy in the Department of African & African Diaspora Studies at the University of Wisconsin-Milwaukee. She is a political scientist who specializes in Black politics, discrimination, and social policies. She published the book *The Politics of Blackness: Racial Identity and Political Behavior in Contemporary Brazil* (Cambridge University Press, 2018). Her current project focuses on the political opinions of Black women social welfare beneficiaries in the United States and Brazil. She has published articles in numerous peer-reviewed journals including *Politics, Groups, and Identities* and the *National Political Science Review*.

Alexandra Nicome lives and works in Minneapolis. She has worked as an interpretation fellow at the Walker Art Center and interned at the Minneapolis Institute of Art, Allen Memorial Art Museum, and National Museum of African Art, Smithsonian Institution. In her work, she uses language to facilitate diverse entry points to art and its contexts.

Njaimeh Njie is a photographer, filmmaker, and multimedia producer. Her work chronicles contemporary Black experiences, with a focus on the connections between place, time, and identity. Njie's work has earned coverage and been featured in outlets including CityLab, Belt Magazine, and the Carnegie Museum of Art's Storyboard blog. Among several awards and grants, Njie was named the 2019 Visual Artist of the Year by the Pittsburgh City Paper, and the 2018 Emerging Artist of the Year by the Pittsburgh Center for the Arts. Njie earned her B.A. in Film and Media Studies in 2010 from Washington University in St. Louis.

Mikael Chukwuma Owunna (b. 1990) is an award-winning queer Nigerian-Swedish American artist, photographer, Fulbright Scholar and engineer born and raised in Pittsburgh, Pennsylvania. Mikael's work explores the relationship between engineering, optics, the black body and queerness. His work has exhibited across Asia, Europe and North America and been featured in media ranging from the *New York Times*, CNN, NPR, BuzzFeed to *Teen Vogue*. Mikael has spoken and lectured about his work at venues including World Press Photo (Netherlands), Harvard Law School, Columbia Law School, Duke University, the Paris Institute of Political Studies (France) and Sveriges Radio (Sweden).

Mary Pattillo is the Harold Washington Professor of Sociology and African American Studies at Northwestern University. She is the author of two award-winning books—*Black Picket Fences* and *Black on the Block*—that explore the entanglements of racial and class inequities in neighborhoods, schools, housing, and crime and policing. She is originally from Milwaukee, WI. Apart from a stint in New York for college, and a couple years abroad, she has lived in the Black Midwest her entire life.

Courtney Wise Randolph is a Detroit Lover with an affinity for hearing and sharing the stories that make and shape who we are. When she's not working at 826michigan inspiring school-aged students to become the writers they want to be, she is daring herself to be the writer she always dreamt to be. She's also a budding podcaster building her audio storytelling skills as an inaugural WDET StoryMakers Fellow.

A writer and educator born and raised in rural southeast Texas, grown by St. Louis, MO, and cultivated in Columbus, OH, **Deva Rashed-Boone** earned her undergraduate degree in African and Afro-American Studies, with a minor concentration in Women's Studies, from Washington University in St. Louis. While Ohio is the sole historically "free state" in which she has lived, the only truly free states she has encountered to date are merely states of mind stemming from her love of her Faith, words, education, children, Afrodescendants throughout the Diaspora, women of color, and other marginalized people.

Katherine Simóne Reynolds' practice is working in emotional dialects and psychogeographies of Blackness the "non," and the importance of "anti-excellence." Her work tries to physicalize emotions and experiences by constructing pieces that include portrait photography, video works, and choreography. In the process of making subtle changes to her practice she has learned that creating an environment built on intention brings the most disarming feelings to her work. Utilizing the Black body and her own personal narrative as a place of departure has made her question her own navigation of ownership, inclusion, and authenticity within a contemporary gaze. She draws inspiration from Black glamour, the Black athlete, and the Church. Her practice generally deals in Blackness from her own perspective and she continually searches for what it means to produce "Black work."

Mark V. Reynolds, a Chicagoan born and raised in Cleveland, has written extensively from the intersection of history, culture, and race as an essayist, journalist, and cultural critic since 1989. He has been a contributor to *Popmatters.com* since 2004, and in 2005 received an Ohio Society of Professional Journalists award for media criticism in *Urban Dialect* magazine. Additional credits include the Cleveland *Plain Dealer, Cleveland Free Times,* and *Black Meetings & Tourism* magazine. His essay, "Race and Kindness in Yellow Springs, OH" was published in the Belt Publishing anthology *Red State Blues: Stories from Midwestern Life on the Left* (2018).

Jamala Rogers is a veteran organizer with deep roots in the Black Liberation Movement. Her battlefronts are wherever her people are, including mass incarceration, police terrorism, reproductive justice, and youth development. Rogers is a poet and prolific writer. She has featured columns on three media platforms: BlackCommentator.com, *Capital City Hues*, and the award-winning *St. Louis American*. She's the author of countless essays and several books, including *Ferguson is America: Roots of Rebellion* (2015). Rogers is faculty for the Black Feminist Organizing School. She is the recipient of numerous community service awards and was the 2017 Organizer-in-Residence at The Havens Center for Social Justice-UW Madison.

Terrence Shambley Jr. (they/them/theirs) is a fiction writer, poet, and facilitator from Saint Paul, Minnesota. They are a college student studying creative writing, philosophy, and their own self-designed major in African American Studies: Radical Imagination. Their work explores the intersections of family, community, and Black life. Some of their work can be found in the 2019 edition of Augsburg University's *Murphy Square,* and TruArtSpeaks' anthology *Dig Deep Be Heard.* Terrence is currently working on their debut novel, which unravels the story of *A'home*—a liberated society founded by escaped African Americans from the 19th century.

Wylliam Smith is a comic book writer and columnist from Grand Rapids, Michigan. In 2019 Smith was named the Iowa Newspaper Association's Master Columnist for his columns published in *The Daily Iowan* newspaper. Currently based in Iowa, Smith focuses his creative work on Black superhero comics while tackling themes of race, sexuality, and male gender norms. Smith is finishing his undergraduate degree at the University of Iowa and freelance writing for the Iowa branch of the National Association of Black Journalists while also writing two comic books.

Melissa N. Stuckey is assistant professor of African American history at Elizabeth City State University in North Carolina. A specialist in early twentieth century black activism, she is author of several magazine and journal articles including "Boley, Indian Territory: Exercising Freedom in the All Black Town," published in 2017 in the *Journal of African American History*. Stuckey is currently completing her first book, entitled *"All Men Up": Race, Rights, and Power in the All-Black Town of Boley, Oklahoma*, which interrogates the black freedom struggle in Oklahoma as it took shape in the state's largest all-black town.

My name is **Zuggie Tate** (she/her/they/them) which is my current name. I am a Black 26 years old, larger-bodied, non-binary fem/AMAB who lives with HIV. I was raised in Cleveland my whole life and attended college in Cleveland as well. I consider myself to be an artist in many ways, but my favorite outlet is definitely poetry. I write as a means of saying the things I'm afraid to say aloud, and share those words with others so that they lose their power over me. My ultimate hope is that in doing so, I give someone else the words they need to fight their demons.

Vanessa Taylor is a writer based in Philadelphia, although Minnesota will always be home. Through articles, essays, fiction, and more, she focuses on Black Muslim womanhood and technology. She is a 2019 Echoing Ida cohort member and the Editor-in-Chief of *The Drinking Gourd*, a Black Muslim literary magazine.

The combination of being a documentary photographer and collage artist has given **Rachel Elise Thomas** the ability to uniquely illustrate and personalize the stories that she tells. Similar to a puzzle, she pieces components together to create a whole that's personalized to her subject matter. She gathers inspiration from their surroundings and interests. Having a background in fine art has allowed her imagination to reach those depths. Her work centers around identity, celebrating diverse communities and its subcultures.

DeMar Walker is the Artistic Director of Ko-Thi Dance Company & the Ton Ko-Thi Children's Performing Ensemble based in Milwaukee, Wisconsin. As a dance teaching artist, they are trained in Hip Hop/Street, West African & Afro-Caribbean techniques. Since 2014, DeMar has been an Associate Lecturer in the Peck School of the Arts/Department of Dance at the University of Wisconsin-Milwaukee. They have also traveled to Guinea & Senegal, West Africa to participate in international workshops with acclaimed dance artists Youssouf Koumbassa, Patrick Acgony & Alesandra Seutin.

Kim-Marie Walker is a nonfiction and fiction writer recently published in *Literary Hub, Killens Review of Arts and Letters, Our Voices, Our Stories Anthology, Birds Thumb, The Compassion Anthology, Talking Stick, Track Four, NILVX*; and author of '*Zebras from Heaven*', a memoir. A travel memoir about her solo pilgrimage to America's transatlantic slave trade ports, honoring the first footsteps of Middle Passage Africans, is a work in progress. Writing residencies include VONA/Voices Writers Workshop, Rhode Island Writers Colony, and Wildacres Retreat. For more information, please visit www.kimmariewalker.com.

David Weathersby is a filmmaker and the founder of City Vanguard. His past projects include the documentaries *Got the Love, Jazz Occurrence, Thee Debauchery Ball* and *The Color of Art*. His work has been featured on The Africa Channel, WTTW, as well as the Pan African Film Festival, the Roxbury International Film Festival, and the Black Harvest Film Festival. He was awarded a Black Excellence award for best director by the African American Arts Alliance of Chicago and his documentary *Thee Debauchery Ball* won the best feature film at the Black Harvest Film Festival and Chicago South Side Film Festival.

Jordan Weber is a Des Moines-based multi-disciplinary artist/activist who works at the cross section of race and environmental justice. His work has been exhibited at White Box, New York; Union for Contemporary Art, Omaha; Intersect Art Center, St. Louis; Des Moines Art Center; Macalester College, Twin Cities, Smack Mellon, New York; Manifest Justice, Los Angeles; Charlotte Street Foundation; Kansas City; Open Engagement, Chicago. Weber is best known for his deconstructed police vehicles turned community gardens/workout equipment, and recontextualized abandoned structures. Awards and fellowships include Harvard LOEB candidate, A Blade of Grass fellowship NYC, Tanne

Foundation fellow, Des Moines Public Art Foundation fellow, and African American Leadership Fellow.

Terrion L. Williamson is an associate professor of African American & African Studies and American Studies at the University of Minnesota where she also serves as the director of the Black Midwest Initiative. Her first book, *Scandalize My Name: Black Feminist Practice and the Making of Black Social Life*, was published by Fordham University Press in 2017 and explores, in part, the conditions of working-class black life in her hometown of Peoria, Illinois.

Tamara Winfrey-Harris is a writer who specializes in the ever-evolving space where current events, politics and pop culture intersect with race and gender. Her work has appeared in *The New York Times, Cosmopolitan, New York* Magazine, *The American Prospect, Ms.* and other media. She is the author of *The Sisters Are Alright: Changing the Broken Narrative of Black Women in America* (Berrett-Koehler 2015) and the upcoming *Letters to Black Girls*, due out in spring 2021, also from Berrett-Koehler. Learn more about Tamara at TamaraWinfreyHarris.com.

Jeffrey C. Wray is a Professor of Film Studies at Michigan State University and an independent filmmaker. Recent films include *Songs for My Ride Side*, a 2020 half-hour drama, *BLAT! Pack Live*, a 2016 music documentary, and *The Evolution of Bert* (2014), which was nominated for the Roger Ebert Award at the Chicago International Film Festival. His films have screened around the world. Screenplays include *The Soul Singer*, a 2018 Nicholl Academy Award Screenwriting Fellowship Quarterfinalist, and *Eclipse*, a political drama set in the turbulent summer of 1964.

Yvonne was the first poetry editor of two pioneering feminist magazines, *Aphra* and *Ms.*, and has received several awards including NEAs for poetry (1974, 1984) and a Leeway (2003) for fiction (as Yvonne Chism-Peace). She is the author of an epic trilogy: *Iwilla Soil, Iwilla Scourge, Iwilla Rise* (Chameleon Productions). Recent anthologies include: *From the Farther Shore* (Bass River Press), *Home: An Anthology* (Flexible), *Quiet Diamonds 2019 & 2018* (Orchard Street), *161 One-Minute Monologues from Literature* (Smith and Kraus), *Philadelphia Stories, Burningword Journal, Bryant Review, Pinyon, Nassau Review, Bosque Press #8, Foreign Literary Journal #1*. Selected list of online publications at www.iwilla.com.